ENGINEERING FOUNDATIONS THAT SCALE

HOW TO BUILD A COMPANY THAT GROWS WITHOUT LOSING ITS SOUL

JAMIE DEWISPELARE

For rights, permissions, or bulk orders, please contact:
jamie@engineeringfoundationsthatscale.com

The Amazon Endure typeface was designed by 2K/DENMARK in 2025.
Template ID: ST-414D415A-25-A01
Printed in the United States.
ISBN: 978-1-83556-496-7 (Paperback)
ISBN: 978-1-83556-497-4 (Hardback)
ISBN: 978-1-83556-498-1 (eBook)

LETTER TO THE READER

Dear Reader,

You hold in your hands more than a book about business.

This is a guide for founders, builders, and dreamers who know scaling isn't just about growing bigger. It's about growing better.

Too many first-generation companies, especially in professional services, hit an invisible ceiling:

- Teams grow faster than culture.
- Revenue grows faster than leadership depth.
- Complexity grows faster than clarity.

And without realizing it, founders drift from purpose into exhaustion.

Over the last two decades, I've had the privilege of working behind the scenes of some of the most quietly exceptional businesses in the AEC industry.

Not in Silicon Valley.

Not on the covers of business magazines.

But inside architecture and engineering firms and construction companies—businesses built by vision, grit, and a deep commitment to excellence.

As a chief financial officer (CFO) and trusted advisor to founders and executive teams, I've seen what growth looks like on paper—revenues rising, headcount expanding, utilization holding steady. But I've also seen what it looks like when clarity fades, and the soul of a company starts slipping through the cracks.

I've watched founders stare at record-breaking financials while privately wondering if they're still building something they believe in.

I've seen world-class teams unravel under the weight of unclear priorities and good intentions turned into organizational drift.

And I've seen companies hit ceilings because the systems, culture, and leadership habits that got them here couldn't take them further. This book is a response to those moments and my attempt to capture what I've learned walking alongside those leaders.

It's not a blueprint for hypergrowth at any cost.

It's not a call to hustle harder or chase the next shiny metric.

It's a practical, story-driven guide for leaders who want to build something that lasts.

You'll meet Sarah, a fictional founder drawn from the composite traits of real leaders I've worked with. Her journey mirrors what I've seen time and again: the moment when what used to work no longer does. And the courageous, messy, strategic work required to build again, with intention.

Each chapter offers a window into those turning points and the tools I've used in real rooms with real executives, facing real decisions. This isn't theory. It's field-tested leadership for companies that matter.

If you're leading a successful firm and sensing that growth is starting to stretch more than just your margins, that it's testing your culture, clarity, and maybe even your confidence, this book is for you.

And if you're wondering whether it's possible to scale without losing your soul?

I'm here to tell you: Yes. But only if you do it on purpose.

Let's build it together with clarity, with discipline, and without losing what made it matter in the first place.

CONTENTS

The Moment They Almost Burned It All Down

It wasn't a dramatic moment.

No walkouts. No lawsuits. No breaking news.

It was just a quiet Tuesday afternoon. A founder I deeply respected sat across from me in a conference room that smelled faintly of whiteboard ink and over-brewed coffee.

Their firm was a rocket ship—twenty million in revenue, prestigious clients, a waiting list for projects.

And yet "I wake up every day with dread," they said, staring through their coffee. "And the worst part? We're winning. We're just winning the wrong game." In that silence, the self-doubt surfaced: What if I'm no longer meant to run my own company?

That's when I realized growth doesn't just test the company. It tests the soul of the person leading it.

I've spent over two decades helping leaders scale, especially first-generation founders in technical and professional services. Architects. Engineers. Strategists. Designers. Builders. People who didn't inherit a machine but crafted one from scratch, with a little duct tape and a lot of vision.

And then one day, everything gets complicated.

Revenue climbs. So does headcount. The calendar gets fuller. The team gets quieter. Decision-making slows. Firefighting becomes a strategy. Culture gets cloudy. And the founder—brilliant, bold, and well-intentioned—starts to wonder:

"Am I building something I even want to lead anymore?"

Not because they're weak. But because the systems that built the company are now breaking it.

This book was born from those conversations. From those turning points. From the late-night email messages and early morning panic texts. From the unglamorous, unfiltered reality of what scaling actually feels like.

So no, this isn't another book about growth hacks, optimization funnels, or how to 10x your whatever.

It's about how to lead when complexity rises faster than clarity.

It's about how to scale without losing your culture, team, or yourself.

It's about making sure the success you're chasing doesn't erase the reason you started in the first place.

You'll meet Sarah in the next chapter. Through her journey, you'll face the same questions every growing company must eventually answer:

- What future are we really building?
- Who do we need to become to build it?
- What do we have to let go of along the way?

If you're feeling the weight of growth or fearing that success might cost more than you expected, this book is for you.

You don't need a new hustle tactic. You need a foundation that scales.

CHAPTER
01

BUILDING THE BLUEPRINT

The Room Was Heavy

Sarah stood at the front of the conference room in Innovate Engineering's sleek, minimal HQ. She had built this moment. Slides polished. Charts updated. Revenue projections modeled. Thanks to their shiny new artificial intelligence (AI)-powered market intelligence tool, predictive growth heatmaps pulsed confidently from the screen. But she was entirely unprepared for what was about to happen.

She spoke with clarity. She hit every note. The project pipeline was thriving. The team's efficiency scores were strong. They were optimizing, systematizing, scaling.

And yet, the silence that followed was suffocating.

Polite nods. One weak "Makes sense." Greg tapped his pen. Monica inhaled, held it, and said nothing. There was no rejection. No spark. No follow-up questions. But no buy-in either.

Sarah stood still as the last laptop closed, and chairs scooted back. The hum of the HVAC filled the vacuum. Behind her, brilliant but bloodless slides still glowed.

She had delivered a plan. What she hadn't delivered was belief.

The Belief Signal Effect

When leaders present a strategy rich in logic but absent of emotional resonance, teams don't object; they disengage. It's not resistance. It's belief decay.

According to Cognitive Load Theory, when people are overloaded with detail, the brain defaults to shortcuts: go along quietly, delay action, or wait for someone else to lead.[1] But belief is a different engine. It runs on clarity, identity, and meaning, not just data.

Sarah's plan was sharp. But it was emotionally silent. It lacked the one thing strategy alone can't generate: a sense of purpose.

And in leadership, emotion is a critical signal, not fluff. It's the story people tell themselves about why they care enough to follow.

---

1   John Sweller, "Cognitive Load During Problem Solving: Effects on Learning," *Cognitive Science* 12, no. 2 (1988): 257–285.

When Logic Isn't Leadership

That's what hurt the most. Not the indifference, but the fact that she couldn't blame anyone for it.

Sarah didn't leave that meeting feeling defeated. She left confused. The logic was sound. The opportunity was clear. The risks, addressed. But as she stood outside the office, the realization hit: She'd built a plan, not belief.

She hadn't given them direction. She'd handed them data. One that made sense to her, the forecast, and the spreadsheet. But not to the people whose hands and hearts would be responsible for executing it.

The Illusion of Agreement

When leaders mistake silence for alignment, they fall into "false consensus," a cognitive trap where we assume others agree because they don't object. But in reality, they're often disoriented, disengaged, or simply unsure how to respond.

She wrote in her notebook: "Why do we exist, beyond projects and profit?"

Then she stared at that question for twenty minutes.

Hustle Builds the Company; Vision Builds the Team

Every founder hits this moment, usually without realizing it until it's too late.

At the start, hustle is everything. But eventually, it becomes an anchor. The team grows, and hustle turns into friction. You're growing, and the numbers look good. The dashboards say you're efficient.

But internally? Meetings feel like checklists. Your best people seem a little flatter. You feel busy, but not bold.

This is founder drift, the creeping dissonance between why you started this company and what you're now scaling. And the worst part? It's often reinforced by your own tools and behavior.

That new AI resource management platform? It's helping you optimize people like puzzle pieces. The automated dashboard? It's reinforcing surface metrics that look good in board meetings but say nothing about meaning. The client sentiment software? It's only as good as the signals it's told to check.

You're making decisions faster than ever. But direction? That's quietly gone missing.

Dopamine Drives Direction

Human motivation runs on a neurochemical loop. When we see a clear purpose, one that feels emotionally real, our brains release dopamine. That's what sustains effort, curiosity, and resilience and drives you forward toward the result with passion.

When that clarity is missing? We default to habits. We simply perform the motions we've been taught. We still hit the metrics and check the boxes, but stop caring. That's not burnout; it's belief decay.

And Sarah was seeing the first cracks forming in her leadership team.

The Vision Pyramid

Draw a pyramid with three stacked layers: top, middle, and bottom. Fill it out yourself with your understanding of how you are driving the fundamentals of the company.

Team Alignment Test: Ask three leaders to complete the same pyramid, without collaboration. Compare your answers.

Pyramid Layer	Focus
Vision	What future are we building?
Strategy	How do our services, structure, and focus get us there?
Values	What do we refuse to compromise, even under pressure?

Vision Versus Vibration

Sarah regrouped. She didn't pitch again; instead, she taught the Vision Pyramid.

Then she asked, "What future are we building?"

Person	Answer	Alignment
Monica	"Efficiency and dependability"	Tactical

Person	Answer	Alignment
Raj	"Helping communities grow smart"	Closer
Greg	"Best-in-class project delivery"	Operational
Jordan	"Solving design problems at scale"	Abstract
Sarah	"Shaping infrastructure that strengthens lives"	Clear

If your leaders can't echo a form of your vision in their own words? You don't have alignment. You have vibration and a lot of movement, but no unified melody. That's where the real work begins.

The AI Decision That Nearly Cost Her the Culture

Two quarters earlier, Sarah had rolled out an AI-powered workforce optimization platform that delivered real-time project allocation. Forecasts were based on delivery speed, availability, and margin targets.

On paper, it was perfect. And for a few weeks? It was perfect. Deliverables sped up, deadlines were easily met, and utilization rates hit an all-time high.

Then Monica stopped speaking up in meetings. Team leads began quietly reassigning junior staff just to stay ahead of the algorithm. The culture started to feel tight.

Sarah got her first real clue when one of the interns, a rising star, skipped the team happy hour and said, "Feels like the system already decided who matters. Not much point in showing up."

Algorithm Aversion

Studies show that when people feel decisions are made by a system instead of for a purpose, engagement drops, even if outcomes improve.[2]

People don't resist tech; they resist meaninglessness.

The system had optimized output. But it had also begun to strip away ownership.

---

2   William A. Kahn, "Psychological Conditions of Personal Engagement and Disengagement at Work," *Academy of Management Journal* 33, no. 4 (1990): 692–724.

Sarah quietly phased it back into "advisory" mode. Not because the software was flawed, but because her clarity was.

The Architect and the Tower

Imagine two architects. One builds fast—skyscraper speed, optimized for market timing. Floors rise weekly.

The other? Slower, studying the land. Sketching, revising, and asking: Who is this for? What will it mean in fifty years?

Three years later, both towers stand. One is taller. The other is an iconic masterpiece. Which do you think will be on an architectural tour or written into history?

You can't automate vision, and you can't rush meaning. AI can accelerate your plan, but if it lacks purpose, it builds regret faster.

The Danger of Data-Driven Drift

Your systems will happily scale whatever you tell them—more projects, output, and client touchpoints. But what are they scaling toward?

The more data you collect, the more confident you become, even when you're headed in the wrong direction. That's data overconfidence bias. You feel momentum, but momentum is not mission.

If your dashboards are blinking green while your people feel gray, that's your signal. Don't zoom in. Zoom out.

Rebuilding Belief

Sarah didn't call an all-hands meeting. She started smaller. She gathered her leads and asked them one question: "What would break your heart to stop doing here?"

The answers surprised her.

"Designing with empathy."

"Mentoring juniors."

"Standing up for smarter public spaces."

She realized the culture hadn't eroded; it had just gone underground. Waiting. Waiting for a signal that it still mattered.

She gave them one. And then she rewrote the blueprint. This time, it wasn't for revenue but resonance.

The Pre-Scale Clarity Checklist

Ask these questions now, not when the culture is already broken:

- What do we believe AI can't replicate?
- Are we building a business worth optimizing, or just something that's easy to measure?
- When I leave the room, do my leaders still make values-driven decisions?
- Are we confusing software-driven efficiency with mission-driven effectiveness?
- If we paused growth for ninety days, would the culture strengthen or crumble?

Closing Reflection

Back at that same kitchen table, Sarah opened her notebook and wrote: "We don't need to scale faster. We need to scale clearer." Because clarity isn't a leadership luxury; it's a survival strategy.

It's especially true now when tools can do more, move faster, and take you further than ever in the wrong direction, if you're not careful.

She made a decision that night. She wouldn't just lead with strategy. She'd lead with soul because AI might run the system. But only clarity builds belief.

In this opening chapter, we've touched on several ideas that we'll unpack further as we go.

This isn't a step-by-step manual or a workbook you can skim through.

My hope is that you'll stop along the way, reflect, and notice how these concepts echo in your own story. They only gain power when you connect them to your real-world experiences.

So, let's dive in together.

CHAPTER
02

SCALING STRESS, FINDING SOUL

The Sunday After

Sarah sat at her kitchen table again. This time, she didn't bring her laptop, just a half-full mug of coffee, a few scattered printouts, and a pad of yellow paper she hadn't touched in months.

This was the first weekend in a while she hadn't scheduled a leadership offsite or checked in with her chief operations officer (COO).

Instead, she was staring at a single sentence she'd scrawled the night before:

"We are scaling stress."

The line hit her like a confession.

Deep down, she already knew: Innovate was expanding. Hiring. Booking larger jobs. Licensing new tools. But it didn't feel stronger. It felt shakier.

More brittle. Less joyful. Like every "win" had a silent cost. Like each new process made the team more cautious, not more confident.

The Growth Illusion

It's a common founder trap: assuming that more work, people, and systems mean progress. But in reality? Most growth strategies are just well-dressed stress multipliers.

Every new hire without alignment introduces complexity. Every client win without clarity introduces risk. Every tech implementation without trust just makes disconnection harder to detect, until it's too late.

Studies in organizational behavior confirm this blind spot. Founders chronically overestimate the benefits of growth and underestimate its cognitive toll. It's called growth bias, which is the assumption that more automatically means better.[3]

More projects. More people. More tools. More visibility.

It looks like momentum, but rarely does anyone stop to ask: More of what? And for whom?

---

3   Frederick P. Brooks Jr., *The Mythical Man-Month: Essays on Software Engineering* (Boston: Addison-Wesley, 1975).

Growth doesn't just scale capacity. It scales everything, including complexity, emotional fatigue, decision velocity, and cultural drift. And often, it does so quietly.

Growth bias overvalues expansion while undervaluing the cost of coordination, communication, and care that must rise in tandem but rarely does.

Founders often chase volume as proof of progress. But volume without meaning is noise. And expansion without clarity is drift. You can end up celebrating numbers while wondering why your culture feels increasingly lifeless.

The illusion? Growth is visible. Its costs are not.

Your dashboards won't show disconnection. Your forecasts won't highlight fragmentation. Your key performance indicators (KPIs) will say more, while your team quietly feels less.

And that's the paradox: growth is only sustainable if you understand its weight. Not just what it adds, but what it asks.

So, the real question becomes: Is your growth building energy? Or is it borrowing it?

When Clarity Becomes a Cage

Clarity isn't just a leadership trait. It's a stabilizer. And when it's missing? Leaders don't slow down; they overcompensate.

When the purpose gets foggy, the structure rushes in. More meetings, dashboards, and frameworks, born from survival. We try to do more when we can't say why.

But structure without meaning doesn't create momentum. It creates a cage. A heavy grid of policies, permissions, and performance reviews that look official but feel hollow.

People don't feel supported. They feel managed. And being managed without knowing what it's all in service of breeds quiet resistance. Not defiance, just disengagement.

Sarah saw the signs. Hallway conversations vanished, email chains replaced whiteboards, and the team clung to deliverables while quietly retreating from the "why."

It wasn't burnout. Not yet. It was something subtler: clarity anxiety. That creeping discomfort when no one can quite explain where the company is going, but everyone's too busy to ask.

So, the rituals of reflection disappeared. Sure, the workflow was polished. The meetings were documented. But no one asked:

What matters most right now?

When clarity goes missing, the process takes over. And without intention, the process becomes performance. Until one day, someone finally asks:

"Why are we even doing it this way?"

And no one has a good answer.

That's the danger. Not that people stop caring, but that they stop believing it matters.

The Algorithm That Forgot the Humans

A few months earlier, Innovate launched an AI-assisted scheduling platform. It promised balance: better workload distribution, fewer burnout cases, optimized utilization. Technically, it worked.

Yet, in practice, it erased one of the team's most human rituals of deciding together who would take on what work, and why.

Before, project assignments were moments of connection. Leaders asked, "Who's curious about this?" or "Who hasn't had a shot at leading lately?" After? The system decided.

More efficient. Less alive.

Within two weeks, Sarah saw the pattern:

- Leaders stopped mentoring juniors.
- Team members stopped offering ideas.
- Everyone became "fine."

She hadn't meant to flatten autonomy, but she had. The algorithm solved for delivery but it ignored dignity.

According to Self-Determination Theory, teams need three things to stay motivated: autonomy, mastery, and purpose. Strip away autonomy, and the rest starts to collapse.[4]

---

4   Edward L. Deci and Richard M. Ryan, "The 'What' and 'Why' of Goal Pursuits: Human Needs and the Self-Determination of Behavior," *Psychological Inquiry* 11, no. 4 (2000): 227–268.

And that's what happened. Before, people raised their hands. Now, they accepted whatever landed in their inbox quietly, politely, and mechanically.

Because when you don't choose the game, even winning it feels like an obligation.

And purpose? That's the most fragile of all. Without agency, it starts to sound like propaganda, or at best, a story told at you, not one built with you.

The system wasn't broken. But the belief was.

Systems may guide action.

But only autonomy inspires ownership.

Not Another Mission Statement

Sarah hated mission statements. Or rather, she hated what they were at most companies: vague, poster-board prose that sounded inspirational until you actually tried to use it.

"Empowering communities through innovative infrastructure solutions."

She'd seen a dozen versions. Heck, Innovate had one on the website.

But when a junior engineer once asked, "What does that actually mean for my work this week?", Sarah didn't have an answer. That was the moment she realized they had a statement, but not a Vision.

A Vision isn't a sentence. It's a spine. And if you don't have one, your culture will borrow someone else's.

The Culture That Builds Itself (If You Don't)

Every organization has a culture. It's not optional. It's not a slide. And it's not always the one you think you have.

Culture is what people do when you're not in the room. It's the logic they use when there isn't a process. It's the decision they make when nobody's watching.

And without a unifying Vision, culture defaults to convenience, politics, or fear.

Every team mirrors the strongest signals in the room. Not the mission statement, but the lived values. The unspoken incentives. The behaviors that get rewarded.

This is what is called a mirror culture. If speed gets praise, people rush. If silence is safer than honesty, consensus appears without conviction. Culture doesn't disappear; it drifts. Not because people stop caring. But because they stop knowing what matters.

Culture isn't declared. It's demonstrated. Over time. Under pressure. And one decision at a time.

The Vision Compass

That night, Sarah grabbed a napkin and wrote four questions. She would later call this her Vision Compass.

Direction	Question
North	What future are we building, not just in outputs but outcomes?
East	Who benefits from our work: clients, communities, or just us?
South	What values will we never compromise, even under pressure?
West	What risks do we refuse to ignore, even if they're profitable?

She tested it on herself first. The answers were foggy. Which meant the direction was, too.

The Culture "Pulse" Meeting

It was the end of Q1, and turnover had started to tick up. Nothing dramatic, but enough to trigger a gut check.

Sarah scheduled a "Culture Pulse." It was a forty-five-minute meeting with the leadership team—no agenda, just a starting prompt:

"What do we believe here that other firms don't?"

Silence.

Then Monica finally said, "That we should care more."

Raj added, "That planning for people matters more than planning for budgets."

After a pause, Greg said, "That we don't have to be the biggest to be the best."

She continued on with a second question:

"What's the one thing we've lost that you wish we could bring back?"

They answered slowly. Carefully. Then the floodgates opened.

- "Time to teach."
- "Permission to challenge the plan."
- "Space to think without filling out a form first."

They weren't asking to move slower. They were asking to matter more.

That was the moment Sarah realized something beautiful, and something terrifying.

They did have a culture. A good one. A powerful one.

But it wasn't being reinforced. It was living off memory.

Vision Isn't a Tagline; It's a Tool

That afternoon, Sarah sketched a draft Vision statement, but not the kind you print.

She called it the Project Filter Vision:

"Innovate exists to design the built environment for human well-being where every project strengthens the community it touches."

She ran it through a test:

- Could a project manager use it to choose between two vendors?
- Could a designer use it to justify an idea?
- Could the business development team use it to decline a lead?

If yes, then it passed.

What Gets Asked, Gets Answered

Sarah realized the collaboration tools were smart, but soulless. The "Engagement Score" tab in their project management/customer relationship management/artificial intelligence (PM/CRM/AI) system reads like this:

- "Responded to all emails within Service Level Agreement (SLA)."
- "Checked in weekly."
- "Maintained communication chain of custody."

Not one note about trust, creativity, or growth.

It was a perfect mirror of the wrong measures. So, Sarah added questions to every internal feedback cycle:

- "What part of this project challenged your creativity?"
- "Did this work allow you to live our Vision?"
- "Would you be proud to tell your family about this outcome?"

Because teams track what leadership appears to care about, if your systems never ask about purpose, people stop prioritizing it.

That doesn't mean they don't want it; they simply don't believe it matters anymore.

The Four Belief Builders

Sarah knew she couldn't just give inspiring talks to rebuild culture at scale. She needed repeatable behavior, embedded in systems.

She focused on four:

- Story: Teams don't remember numbers. They remember moments. They started celebrating moments where Vision was lived.
- Symbol: They designed a new internal recognition badge, named "Built to Last." It would be given monthly to someone who chose long-term impact over short-term gain.
- System: She integrated values-based filters into AI dashboards. If a project trended red but had a high community impact, it was flagged for a conversation, not just a correction.
- Standard: Vision became part of every performance review: "In what ways did you model our Vision this quarter?"

The Values Fit Checklist

Question	Yes/No
Does this client respect our time and team boundaries?	☐ Yes
	☐ No
Will this project allow us to lead, not just serve?	☐ Yes
	☐ No
Is the end result something we'll be proud of?	☐ Yes
	☐ No
Are we taking this because we're aligned, or afraid to say no?	☐ Yes
	☐ No

The Culture-driven Decision

Two months later, a new client prospect came in with a large scope, high budget, and a known reputation for burning out vendors.

The business development team was tempted.

Sarah reviewed the scope. Everything made sense, technically. But nothing aligned emotionally.

So, she asked her team, "What does our culture say about this?"

They said no to the project to protect the culture. Together.

That moment became a team story.

One they still tell.

Because culture becomes real not when it's written, but when it's tested.

Closing Reflection

Sarah now began every quarter with a simple question to her team:

"What are we here to build, not just deliver?"

The answers didn't all match word-for-word.

But they rhymed. They resonated. That was the goal.

Because Vision isn't an announcement. It's the container your culture grows inside.

And if you don't build it?

Something else will.

CHAPTER
03

THE ILLUSION OF INDISPENSABILITY

The Meeting She Couldn't Walk Into

Sarah circled the lot. Once. Twice. A third time, slower. Not because she couldn't find a parking space. There were plenty. But because she couldn't make herself pull in.

This wasn't just any meeting. It was the first Vision Activation workshop she had personally initiated. A turning point for her company. The kind of thing she used to lead with energy, with certainty.

But now? She sat idling in her car, the engine humming, hand resting on the door handle, frozen. Seventeen minutes late. Not by accident, but by dread.

Inside that building, her team was already gathered. They had the decks. They the strategy. They had the tools. And for the first time, she wasn't sure if they still needed her to make any of it work.

That thought hit hard, not as a dramatic crisis, but as a quiet unraveling. It wasn't just control that Sarah feared losing. It was relevance.

She wasn't afraid of stepping back from the day-to-day. She was afraid of disappearing altogether.

This company, every inch of it, had been shaped by her judgment, instincts, and grit. From the earliest design proposals to the biggest pitches, she had been the thread that held it all together.

Letting go now didn't feel like empowerment. It felt like erasure.

Even worse: the business was thriving. Deadlines were being hit. Clients were satisfied. The team was solving problems without her. Everything she had worked for was finally happening without her.

That was the moment the panic crept in. What if I'm not essential anymore? And if I'm not essential, who am I here?

She didn't know the answer. But she knew something needed to change. Because the fear wasn't coming from the business falling apart, it was coming from the possibility that it no longer depended on her to hold it together.

The Bottleneck Is the Person Who Got You Here

Founders start as the motor. But over time, those same instincts become the constraint.

Symptom	Root Problem
Final say on all decisions	Lack of trust, no systems
Fixing more than coaching	No role clarity
Calendar full, progress fuzzy	No delegation pipeline

The Addictive Pull of Control

Every founder has something they unconsciously treat as sacred.

For Sarah, it was the final say on scopes over $500K. The design language had to be right. The margin had to make sense. She'd say it was about quality, but the real reason was that it made her feel like the company still ran on her instincts.

Control wasn't just a habit. It was a fix. Every task reviewed. Every decision was weighed in on. Every update cc'd. They were all tiny affirmations that she mattered.

She told herself it was about maintaining standards, protecting the brand, and ensuring alignment.

But really? It was about staying central.

Control Addiction

Control addiction doesn't look like micromanagement.

It looks like "I'm just being thorough."

It sounds like "I'll give it one last look."

It hides under "I just want to make sure it's right."

But underneath? It's fear.

Fear of being left out.

Fear of being unnecessary.

Fear of irrelevance.

Founders overestimate the risk of delegation and underestimate the cost of control. It's called the illusion of indispensability, a deeply human bias that convinces us our involvement is always additive. But the math doesn't check out.

When you do what others should? They don't learn how.

When you correct instead of coaching? They don't grow.

When everything flows through you? You become the bottleneck you swore you'd never be.

What Control Is Actually Costing You

Control Feels Like	But Actually Means
"Protecting quality"	Lack of training or clear expectations
"Being responsible"	Avoidance of leadership development
"Ensuring nothing breaks"	Unwillingness to share risk
"Still being involved"	A fear of no longer being needed
"Just helping out"	A dependency loop that disempowers

Letting Go with Purpose

That afternoon, Sarah blocked off an hour and sat down with a yellow legal pad. She drew three columns.

Then, one by one, she walked through the list with Daniel and Monica, not with fear, but with resolve.

"This isn't about stepping away," she said. "It's about building the kind of company that doesn't break when I step back."

The Let-Go Ledger

I Still Control	I Could Teach	I Must Let Go
Final pitch reviews	Budget planning	Paid time off (PTO) approvals
High-stakes scopes	Hiring strategy	Scheduling
Client fire drills	Conflict handling	Daily standups

They started to use this every quarter in leadership syncs or solo reflections.

They chose one from each column to move forward and invited feedback along the way.

This began the era of coaching through discomfort and celebrating the shift.

The Confidence Audit

Her calendar used to feel like proof of value. Every hour booked. Every crisis escalated. Every touchpoint managed.

But looking back, she realized the truth. A full calendar isn't a sign of leadership. It's a sign of dependency.

Because if your systems rely on your presence to work? You don't have systems. You have founder-shaped duct tape.

Sarah started a simple weekly habit. Every Friday, she asked herself four questions:

Control	Response
What did I touch this week that someone else could have owned?	Two scopes. One budget decision.
What did I fix instead of coaching through?	A client handoff issue.
What decision did I override? Why?	Project timeline pushback that wasn't urgent, just familiar.
What did I fear would fail without me and didn't?	The business development (BD) team's client meeting. They crushed it.

That last one? She underlined twice.

Founder Identity Versus Founder Evolution

Letting go isn't about losing relevance. It's about shifting from being the engine to the architect. And architects don't pour every slab of concrete. They design the foundation that holds the weight.

Sarah's new mantra became: "I'm not the system. I build the system."

To help her team do the same, Sarah drew a leadership loop on the whiteboard: Coach → Empower → Review → Release.

Then came the hard questions:

- Are you teaching principles or just fixing problems?
- Are you building judgment or giving instructions?

- Can your team succeed without you and know you're proud of them?

It wasn't easy. But it was clarifying.

For deeper reflection, Sarah began asking her leaders and herself a simple but unsettling question:

"If I disappeared for six months, what would stop working?"

The answers exposed control triggers disguised as responsibilities.

That's where the real work begins.

Closing Reflection

Sarah didn't become less essential. She became more strategic.

Her team didn't need her less. They trusted themselves more.

True leadership isn't about being the hero in the room. It's about building rooms that don't need one.

CHAPTER
04

PEOPLE BEFORE PROCESS

The Autopilot Trap

Two months into Innovate's growth sprint, things were moving quickly.

Sarah had finally done what she used to dream about; she no longer had to make every decision. Her directors had autonomy. Her PMs had structure. Their AI-enhanced workflow tool hummed with assignments, check-ins, and updated timelines.

From the outside, it looked like leadership was scaling. But something was off.

Her team was hitting deadlines. Client feedback was solid. Revenue was ahead of the forecast.

Yet Sarah felt removed. Not uninvolved. But untethered.

Like she was watching her company succeed through a pane of soundproof glass.

Control Recalibration

Founders often experience identity dissonance when their control diminishes before meaning deepens.

You can delegate tasks, but if trust hasn't taken root, progress feels more like a threat than a relief.

Sarah wasn't micromanaging anymore, but something still felt wrong.

The signal came during a team retrospective. The AI dashboard flagged issues. There were missed inspections, revised deadlines, and a surprise client restraint.

Monica said, "We resolved them using SOP 5C."

Raj added, "The escalation workflow worked. Everything's back on track."

And it was, at least technically.

But no one mentioned who felt the pressure, who showed up, and who improvised. The system had solved the problems. But the people had gone missing.

They weren't leading; they were complying. Sarah realized they were optimizing for execution, not experience.

The Erosion of the Human Margin

Every company has a human margin: the invisible emotional buffer that allows teams to absorb pressure without splintering. Built through trust, recognition, and shared purpose, it lets teams stretch without snapping.

But systems and processes, if over-applied, quietly erode that margin. They don't ask who's tired or drifting; they just move forward.

One system in particular made this painfully clear: their AI-powered proposal generator.

It was fast, efficient, and data-driven. But it removed the humans from the loop.

Designers didn't shape proposals anymore; they inherited them.

"I used to feel like I was building something," one told Sarah.

"Now I just feel like I'm fulfilling it."

The system hadn't failed. It had just forgotten what made the work matter.

Disempowered by Design

Most systems start with good intentions. Built to make things smoother, smarter, faster. And at first, they do. They reduce chaos. Increase predictability. Create the illusion that things are running effortlessly.

But if those same systems strip away voice, autonomy, or judgment? They don't scale efficiency. They scale disengagement.

At Innovate, Sarah had watched this unfold slowly. Proposal generators. Scheduling tools. Performance dashboards. None of them were wrong, and none were maliciously designed. But each had quietly shifted decisions further away from the people actually doing the work.

The result? A team that followed instructions. But stopped feeling involved.

Remember, people are motivated by three psychological nutrients: autonomy, mastery, and purpose. Take away one, even with good intentions, and you don't just slow growth. You sever meaning. Work becomes transactional. People comply instead of contributing. They check boxes—not because they're lazy, but because the system has stopped inviting them to think.

The system was running. But the people were drifting.

Sarah realized her firm hadn't broken anything. It had simply forgotten someone essential: the human being.

No system, no matter how well designed, should replace reflection. No dashboard should dull the instinct to care. And no automation should be so efficient that it erases the reason people chose this profession in the first place.

When systems become too rigid, they don't just make work easier. They make people feel smaller.

One designer put it perfectly in a retrospective: "I used to feel like I was designing communities. Now I just execute workflows."

That hit Sarah hard. Because the work hadn't changed, but the experience of doing it had.

So, she made a decision: systems would stay, but not without soul. Every tool had to answer a new question: Does this encourage better thinking, or just faster clicking?

You can't build a company on autopilot and expect it to feel alive.

The Audit That Changed Everything

Sarah blocked two hours and did something she hadn't done in years: she printed every internal process document and laid them on the floor.

Dozens of them, each originally designed to solve a problem. She color-coded them: green for systems that empowered people, yellow for neutral, and red for those that replaced judgment.

Nearly forty percent were red. Not because they were broken, but because they prioritized speed over strength.

That moment shifted her mindset.

She wrote on the whiteboard above her desk: "No process should remove the need for leadership. It should increase the opportunity for it."

From that point forward, every process had to answer two questions:

- Does this empower judgment or replace it?
- Does this support team growth or shortcut it?

The team began rebuilding by looping designers into proposal development before automation took over. They replaced ticket-based escalations with quick, live huddles and added human context to dashboard alerts so stories didn't disappear behind red flags.

These weren't tweaks. They were invitations to lead again.

When Systems Silence the Soul

Research shows teams are most resilient when systems don't just standardize action, they reinforce identity.[5]

When people feel seen and consulted, they don't just comply. They commit.

But many founder-led firms fall into the same trap: they start using tools to replace conversations.

What begins as streamlining ends as silencing.

Dashboards bring real-time clarity. Workflows run without supervision. Automation replaces repetition.

At first, it feels like progress. In some ways, it is. But slowly, dangerously, something shifts.

The team stops asking, "Why are we doing this?" and starts asking, "Did the system log it?"

Curiosity gives way to compliance. Reflection is outsourced to whatever the dashboard recommends.

The Cost of Scaling Without Soul

Sarah saw it unfold firsthand. Innovate's scheduling tool began auto-assigning roles with eerie accuracy.

It was efficient. But the side effect? Conversations vanished. No more huddles about stretch assignments or routine fatigue.

The tool did its job while the culture paid the price.

---

5   Ming Fan, Wei Cai, and Lin Jiang, "Can Team Resilience Boost Team Creativity among Undergraduate Students? A Sequential Mediation Model of Team Creative Efficacy and Team Trust," *Frontiers in Psychology* 12 (2021): 604692.

The moment a system replaces reflection, you've automated your way into disconnection. And disconnection always hides before it hurts.

The metrics stay green. The systems hum. But the spark fades.

And one day, someone quietly says, "It just doesn't feel like us anymore."

That's when you realize you didn't outgrow your culture.

You outsourced it.

The truth is that founders don't need to choose between care or clarity, culture or control.

The best systems don't eliminate humanity, they amplify it.

They build a process around people, not over them.

The Behavior Loop That Matters Most

In the next team lead meeting, Sarah shared a simple model: "Process should create confidence, not compliance."

She drew a loop: Purpose → Process → Practice → Pride → Performance → reconnecting back at Purpose.

And then she asked, "Where is your team stuck?"

Most said, "Practice to Pride."

They were doing things well, but not feeling proud. Which meant the process was hollow.

After that meeting, they started ending 1:1s with a new prompt: "What process is stealing your confidence?"

The answers changed everything.

One person cited the task review tool: "Feels like a gradebook." Another said the handoff doc: "Nobody reads it, so I stopped caring." A third mentioned the onboarding flow: "Great checklist. No soul." None of them were whining. They were just craving connection.

The Two Types of Systems

Every system your business uses falls into one of two buckets:

System Type	What It Does	Risk
Empowerment System	Builds skill, confidence, judgment	Slower up front
Extraction System	Increases output, reduces variability	Erodes trust over time

The solution isn't to avoid systems. It's to design them with empathy.

The "Why Map" Process Audit

Sarah created a new review template for any system:

System	Purpose	What belief does this reinforce?	Who benefits most?	When was it last challenged?
AI-powered workforce optimization	Real-time project allocation, and margin targets	Efficiency should drive resourcing	Executives tracking utilization and deadlines	Two quarters ago, when Sarah reverted it to advisory mode
Proposal generator	Automate proposal generation	Speed is more valuable than team input or creativity	Business development	When Sarah reintroduced designers into proposal creation

She had each team audit one system a week. And if a system couldn't answer those questions? It was reworked or removed.

The Client Experience Loop

Interestingly, as internal systems became more human-centered, something else changed: Client experience improved.

Clients started using words like "easy to trust," "flexible," and "thoughtful." Not just "on time" or "accurate."

When teams feel valued, they pass that feeling to clients.

Even your automation is interpreted differently when it comes from an energized, empowered team.

Systems don't just shape internal performance; they shape external perception.

Closing Reflection

Systems are not the enemy. But systems that ignore humanity? That's where good companies go numb.

Sarah realized that leadership isn't about letting go of control. It's about reimagining it.

Not as structure versus soul. But as a structure for the soul.

Because when the process amplifies people, you don't just scale capacity. You scale belief.

CHAPTER

05

LEADING FROM THE MIDDLE

The Cost of Quiet Competence

Monica was brilliant.

Not the kind of brilliant that announces itself. The kind that makes the system look smarter than it is. Deadlines met. Conflict defused. Clients managed. Her team moved like clockwork, and she was the one quietly winding the mechanism.

Which is why no one noticed when she started to bend.

At first, it was small. A deliverable approved without full peer review. A design decision was made to appease a long-standing client, even though it conflicted with the firm's stated values. A junior engineer was reassigned quietly, without explanation, because he was "too much work."

Sarah didn't notice.

Because the numbers looked good, the dashboard showed green, and utilization was stable. And Monica, as always, looked fine.

Until she wasn't.

The Unraveling

It started with a Friday call from a client. Not angry, just confused.

"We got a version of the site plan that doesn't match what we signed off on. Monica said it was approved?"

Sarah called Monica. There was a pause. "Yeah. I made a judgment call. We were late. They'd been dragging their feet. I knew what they'd say anyway."

Sarah asked if the change had been documented. Another pause. "Sort of. I meant to log it."

Silence. This wasn't negligence.

It was something worse. Compensated compromise.

The kind of mistake that comes from someone carrying too much for too long without anyone noticing. Monica wasn't slacking. She was silently absorbing organizational friction and, in the process, compromising her judgment.

Load Versus Leverage

Top performers often suffer silently. Not because they can't handle the load, but because they assume they should. It's a form of invisible labor: the emotional, relational, and untracked work that keeps companies together.

Middle managers like Monica don't complain. They compensate. But over time, compensation collapses.

Sarah wasn't watching failure. She was watching friction that had nowhere to go.

Recognition doesn't just reward behavior. It sustains belief. And in organizations that scale fast, the most dangerous leaks don't show up in the numbers. They show up in the people who stop speaking up.

The Dashboard Paradox

Innovate had a slick leadership dashboard. It tracked task velocity—resourcing conflicts, hours logged, and revenue by project and phase.

It was useful until it became misleading.

Monica always looked fine on paper. No missed deadlines. No team churn. No escalations. But the human story didn't match the data.

Sarah realized that systems were telling her what was happening, not how it felt to make it happen. And that's a dangerous blind spot for any founder.

Leading from the Middle Requires More than Execution

Middle leaders are the culture carriers.

They translate Vision into action. They spot burnout before it becomes turnover. They know when a client is bluffing or a junior is floundering, even when the metrics say otherwise.

But they're also the least supported because they're not struggling enough to be saved or senior enough to be prioritized.

Which means most founder-led firms build their entire culture on the backs of under-empowered middle managers.

Sarah coined a new phrase with her team: the "Belief Budget." It referred to how much emotional energy each leader had left, not for tasks but for belief.

The capacity to inspire. To mentor. To coach. To care. And just like a financial budget, it could go into overdraft, especially when mid-level leaders were managing both up and down.

The Calibration Huddle

She invited her leads into a sixty-minute roundtable. No slides. No agenda. Just a question: "What do you wish the top knew about leading from the middle?"

The responses were raw.

"I wish you saw the coaching we do that doesn't show up on reports."

"I wish you'd ask us what to automate, not assume it."

"I wish we were allowed to question the tools, not just use them."

They weren't resisting innovation. They were resisting invisibility.

Earned Agency

People commit more deeply to systems they've helped shape. It's not just about buy-in; it's about identity. When leaders at any level feel that their voice influenced the structure, the structure starts to feel like theirs. And the inverse is just as true: When change is handed down without their input, even the smartest strategies can land like a mandate.

Middle leaders, especially, often hold quiet resistance, not because they fear change, but because they weren't part of designing it. They see the gaps. They feel friction. Yet they're still expected to roll it out with enthusiasm. The result? Compliance without conviction.

Behavioral research backs this up. The "procedural justice" principle shows that people are more likely to accept even unfavorable outcomes if they believe the process was fair and inclusive.[6] Agency isn't a perk; it's a prerequisite for durable alignment.

---

6   W. Chan Kim and Renée Mauborgne, "Fair Process: Managing in the Knowledge Economy," *Harvard Business Review* 81, no. 1 (2003): 127–136.

Without agency, alignment becomes compliance. And compliance is brittle. It holds under observation, but cracks under pressure. True alignment, the kind that sustains through stress and ambiguity, can only be earned through participation.

Sarah saw this firsthand when she invited her mid-level team into a pre-rollout review of a new resource allocation model. Instead of announcing it, she opened with: "What would make this model easier to trust?" The answers reshaped the system entirely. Not just improving adoption but embedding ownership. Suddenly, the rollout wasn't a directive. It was a shared decision. And that subtle shift turned reluctant implementers into engaged architects.

Earned agency isn't just a leadership tactic. It's a culture multiplier.

It turns delegation into trust, decisions into belief, and change into momentum.

Rethinking Leadership Architecture

Sarah sketched a new model: Innovate would lead from the middle out instead of top-down or bottom-up.

That meant three things:

- Involve middle leaders in strategy before rollout.
- Give them discretion, not just delegation.
- Let them audit the tools, not just teach them.

Trust doesn't scale through hierarchy. It scales through participation.

Sarah asked each leader to document their invisible work to support this shift.

Tasks like:

- Informal coaching
- Conflict diffusion
- Manual process patches
- Early risk spotting
- Culture repair

It was eye-opening.

Some were spending ten to twelve hours a week on untracked but critical tasks. No one had asked them to. But without it, the company wouldn't run.

They realized that some "invisible" work could be supported with better tools, like automated client communications or pre-draft reports.

But much of it was emotional labor that couldn't be outsourced.

Instead, they began rewarding it.

Middle leaders nominated one another each quarter for "cultural impact" wins, not just project wins.

The impact? Morale rose. Retention stabilized. Conflicts decreased.

People perform better when they feel seen, not just used.

AI was still useful. But Sarah realized its role had to shift, from decision engine to decision enhancer.

They trained the system to flag not just late tasks, but also consecutive fifty-plus-hour weeks. It now reassigned auto-generated tasks if someone hadn't had PTO in two months.

The AI didn't create empathy. But it created visibility. And that gave leaders space to lead like humans, not machines.

Leadership Leverage Versus Leadership Leakage

They introduced a new review system:

Leadership Activity	Creates leverage or causes leakage?
Assigning tasks without context	Leakage
Asking mid-levels to enforce unpopular rules	Leakage
Delegating decisions with clear purpose	Leverage
Involving leads in project retro analysis	Leverage

The goal wasn't to reduce effort, but to redirect it toward what compounds value. To make that possible, Sarah empowered her leaders with a clearer way to confidently hand off decisions using a decision matrix.

Decision Type	Who makes it?	Can it be challenged?	Why it matters
Scope deviation	Team Lead	Yes	Builds ownership
Client pushback	PM or Director	Yes	Builds courage
Tool adoption	Team + Tech Ops	Yes	Builds trust
Hiring choice	Team + HR	No	Legal risk

This wasn't about chaos; it was about clarity.

Over six months, Innovate rebalanced the middle, through several initiatives:

- Building a real-time leadership pulse

- Tracking not just deliverables but leader sentiment

- Opening monthly forums to question strategy not as rebellion, but as refinement.

And Sarah? She stopped managing the center. She started listening to it.

Because when people know what they own, they stop bracing and start building.

Closing Reflection

Scaling doesn't just stretch your systems. It stretches your people.

Middle leaders don't break loudly. They bend. Then they snap.

If you're not watching closely, their fall looks like a drop in performance. But it started months earlier in silence, in the skipped 1:1s, and the praise without support.

If you want your company to scale, don't just empower your middle. Protect it. Fortify it. Admit when you've leaned on it too hard.

Brilliance in the middle is not infinite. And when it disappears, you lose more than output.

But if you empower it? Your middle becomes your leadership multiplier.

Real leadership isn't just setting direction from the top. It's listening to the people holding the weight and designing with them, not simply for them.

CHAPTER
06

REDESIGNING
ACCOUNTABILITY

When Everything Works but Trust Wobbles

The following Monday, Sarah walked into the strategy room and sat down without opening her laptop. For once, she didn't need the dashboard to tell her something was off.

She already knew.

Monica's judgment call of quietly altering scope, skipping process, and triggering a client's discomfort had cracked something deeper than protocol.

It wasn't the mistake that caused concern. Those happened all the time and usually got patched with a calm word and a clearer standard operating procedure (SOP). This one was different.

It revealed a fragile trust loop. The company's mid-level leaders weren't just making decisions; they were absorbing ambiguity without support and then being quietly punished when the outcome didn't align with leadership's unspoken expectations.

The accountability system wasn't broken. It was misaligned. It rewarded results but left interpretation up to whoever was willing to carry the emotional cost of risk.

And in Monica's case? That cost had accumulated quietly, like structural fatigue in a beam no one thought to check.

Accountability Isn't What You Think It Is

Sarah used to think accountability meant consequences.

Deadlines missed? Check-ins.

KPIs missed? Escalations.

Team member underperforming? Feedback loop plus thirty-day plan.

She'd inherited that mindset from early mentors. From the project playbooks. From the engineering world itself, where calculations and codes held zero tolerance for drift.

But humans aren't spreadsheets. And if you lead like they are, they'll disengage long before they underperform.

Real accountability isn't about catching people doing things wrong. It's about creating the conditions that help them do things right.

The Accountability Myth

One morning, Sarah overheard a conversation between two junior engineers.

"I'm scared to miss the Thursday check-in," one said. "I always feel like it's a trap."

That phrase stuck in her head for days: a trap. How did they get here? How did accountability turn into anxiety?

Psychological Safety Is a Prerequisite

People don't grow in fear. They grow in safety.

Psychological safety, or the belief that you can speak up, take risks, or admit mistakes without fear of punishment or humiliation, isn't a "soft" concept. It's the core condition for learning, innovation, and accountability that actually sticks.

When teams feel safe, they offer ideas before they're fully baked. They challenge faulty assumptions. They surface early warning signs. They own missteps not only because they have to, but because they trust the environment they're in.

But here's the paradox: most traditional "accountability systems" unintentionally erode that safety by design.

Why? Because they're not built to nurture growth. They're built to detect failure.

Sarah saw this firsthand. Her team had installed an automated progress tracker that flagged delays automatically. The moment a task slipped past its deadline, a red icon blinked. The system was accurate, and ruthlessly so. But it was also emotionally tone-deaf.

The message it sent wasn't "How can we support you?" It was "You're behind!"

Even if no one said it out loud, the emotional climate shifted. Team members stopped reporting early issues. Status updates became sanitized. Reflection was replaced by defensiveness.

And once that shift happens, real accountability collapses. Not visibly, but silently. In the fear-laced pauses before someone speaks. In the unasked question. In the problem that surfaces too late because no one wanted to be "the one who missed something."

Behavioral science confirms this: fear activates the amygdala, the brain's threat center. Once triggered, we narrow our focus, avoid risk, and prioritize self-protection over collaboration. It's the very opposite of what great teams need to thrive.[7]

That's why psychological safety isn't a luxury. It's not a bonus trait for high-functioning teams.

It's the prerequisite for real accountability, or at least the kind that leads to growth, not just compliance.

Because you can't expect people to own the hard things if they're afraid of what ownership will cost.

Redesigning What Accountability Actually Means

Sarah sat down with her leadership team and wrote a new definition on the board: "Accountability is the outcome of shared clarity and mutual trust."

If people weren't meeting expectations, it wasn't just their fault.

It was a failure of shared clarity. Or mutual trust. Or both.

The Old Model Versus the New Model

Model	Focus	Signal	Outcome
Traditional	Blame	Error	Compliance (short-term)
Evolved	Clarity	Misalignment	Growth (long-term)

Accountability wasn't a lever to pull. It was a design decision.

The Accountability-Trust Loop

Most accountability systems unintentionally teach fear, not ownership.

Behavioral science shows that when accountability is tied to surveillance, not support, it activates the brain's threat response. Blame triggers cortisol, narrows perception, and kills learning.[8] People shift into protection mode—avoiding risk, feedback, and even visibility.

---

7   Joseph E. LeDoux, *The Emotional Brain: The Mysterious Underpinnings of Emotional Life* (New York: Simon & Schuster, 1996).
8   Amy C. Edmondson, *The Fearless Organization: Creating Psychological Safety in the Workplace for Learning, Innovation, and Growth* (Hoboken, NJ: Wiley, 2019).

Sarah realized that real accountability isn't enforced, it's enabled. It's not about tracking failure. It's about designing clarity, inviting trust, and building systems where people can tell the truth about what's hard without fear of fallout.

Psychological safety isn't a bonus. It's a prerequisite.

When accountability feels like mutual trust in motion, teams don't hide mistakes; they surface them faster. They don't wait to be corrected; they ask to be supported.

Because when people feel safe, they don't protect their image. They protect the mission.

Where AI Made It Worse, and How They Fixed It

One of their internal systems used an AI engine to flag deliverables that were delayed more than seventy-two hours past estimate. The flag was sent to project leads automatically.

What started as a helpful "heads up" turned into a culture of passive judgment. No one asked why something was late, only who caused it.

The AI was technically right but emotionally tone-deaf. So, they rewrote the workflow.

Now, a delay trigger opens a check-in prompt that asks:

- What has shifted since the estimate?
- What support would help most now?
- What would success look like from here?

Suddenly, those check-ins felt like coaching, not compliance.

Blame Hijacks Learning

Blame doesn't fix behavior. It fractures trust.

When something goes wrong, such as a missed deadline, a misstep in client communication, or a dropped detail in a deliverable, the natural instinct in most organizations is to figure out who's responsible. But when "Who's responsible?" becomes shorthand for "Who's at fault?" we stop learning. And we start protecting.

Neuroscience helps explain why.

When people perceive blame, even subtly, even when unspoken, the brain triggers a threat response. The amygdala fires. The prefrontal cortex that governs reasoning, creativity, and complex problem-solving begins to shut down. The nervous system shifts from reflection into survival.

Fight, flight, freeze, fawn, flop.

Not only does this reaction hinder collaboration, but it also literally shuts off the brain's ability to integrate feedback. You can't grow from a conversation while your entire body braces for judgment.

Sarah saw this pattern surface during project retros. One team member would share a missed task or error, and instead of curiosity, the room tensed. Heads down. Glances exchanged. Nobody asked why. They just quietly took mental notes so they could avoid being the next red flag.

The system wasn't punitive by design. But the behavior it creates? Pure defensiveness.

That's the danger of blame: It disguises itself as accountability but poisons the process.

And once it shows up in a team, even once, people start playing it safe. They over-document. They under-share. They stop asking for help because they've learned that transparency is risky.

But something powerful happens when accountability is reframed and seen as a performance review instead of a learning loop.

Engagement rises.

Ideas re-enter the room.

People stop avoiding ownership and start leaning into it.

Because when a team knows that truth-telling won't lead to punishment, it creates the space for actual growth.

The work gets better, and, most importantly, so do the people.

The Three Layers of Accountability

Sarah started training her managers to think in three layers:

- Personal: "What am I owning?"
- Relational: "Who am I supporting or disappointing?"
- Cultural: "What story am I contributing to?"

If someone misses a deliverable, it's not just about the rework hours. It's about trust. About ripple effects. About momentum.

They started using this three-layer model in project retro meetings. Not as punishment, but as reflection.

The First Accountability Design Session

Sarah brought the team together with a provocative goal:

"Let's design a system that makes people excited to be accountable."

At first, people laughed. Then Monica said:

"What if accountability felt like being trusted?"

And the room got quiet. That became the design constraint: accountability must feel like trust in action.

They created four trust-based practices:

- Self-commitments: Everyone submits one weekly goal that matters to them, not just their team. These get revisited in 1:1s.

- Narrative-based reporting: Instead of "percent complete," team leads write a short narrative update: progress, roadblocks, next steps, and emotional energy level.

- Feedback opt-in: Once a month, each team member chooses one peer and one lead to ask for feedback on their terms.

- Public repair, private resolve: If something breaks trust, the team discusses it in a learning-focused way, but solutions are always delivered one-on-one, never in public.

The result? A massive shift in tone. People weren't defensive. They were reflective.

They weren't hiding. They were sharing.

The Accountability Spectrum

They also mapped where different people landed on what they called the "Accountability Spectrum":

Type	Behavior	Coaching Focus
Avoiders	Downplay, defer, disappear	Build safety & clarity
Performers	Obsess over metrics	Normalize failure

Type	Behavior	Coaching Focus
Owners	Balance action with reflection	Celebrate integrity

This helped managers shift from punishing Avoiders or over-relying on Performers and start developing more Owners.

Why Most Accountability Systems Fail

Most accountability systems fail because they try to impose clarity through structure instead of co-creating it through conversation.

They treat people like nodes, not humans.

Worst of all, they avoid the real work. They don't name where trust is quietly breaking.

At the next leadership offsite, Sarah decided to name it. She opened with a single prompt:

"What's one place where we've been avoiding accountability as a team?"

Greg broke the silence. "We keep renewing that high-revenue client," he said, "but we all know they erode our culture."

The room was quiet. Then came the nods.

Two weeks later, they ended the contract with that client. And the cultural gain far outweighed the financial loss.

Closing Reflection

Accountability isn't a list of rules. It's a signal of trust.

It's not enforced; it's enabled.

And it's not about punishment. It's about pride.

Sarah learned that real accountability isn't what happens when someone drops the ball. It's what happens when everyone knows the game and still chooses to play together.

Because that's what a great team does. Not because they're afraid, but because they care.

CHAPTER
07

SYSTEMS THAT SERVE

When the System Becomes the Story

Sarah sat quietly during the weekly operations review, eyes flicking between the real-time dashboard and the tired faces around the table.

Sarah didn't see the warning signs. Not because they weren't there, but because they were beautifully formatted.

The new AI workflow dashboard had launched six weeks earlier. Designed to optimize resourcing, it pulled in historical performance, role complexity, and utilization targets, then suggested weekly task assignments.

The firm's delivery rate ticked up within days. Fewer bottlenecks. Cleaner reviews. Even the interns were getting praise for "getting ahead of schedule." It looked like a triumph of alignment.

Then Anjali quit.

She didn't send a farewell email. No Teams message. No exit interview.

She left a note on Sarah's desk: "I didn't leave the company. The company left me six weeks ago. I just finally caught up."

Sarah had barely known Anjali. Mid-level designer. Quiet. Dependable. The kind of person the system loved, one with predictable inputs and consistent outputs. But when she started digging, Sarah found the problem.

Anjali had been assigned work at 110% capacity for five straight weeks.

It was a mistake. The AI said she could handle it based on past output, not current context. Anjali had flagged it twice in system comments. Nobody saw them. The AI didn't surface flags, only performance scores.

Sarah asked operations why no one noticed. They showed her the utilization chart. It was green.

That was the moment Sarah realized something chilling: The system wasn't broken. It just didn't care.

At the next leadership meeting, Sarah didn't bring charts. She brought Anjali's note.

She asked everyone to write down one time in the last month they'd overruled their own instincts because a system told them it was "efficient."

Greg admitted he'd delayed a feedback conversation because the coaching tracker hadn't hit its "priority" threshold.

Monica confessed she'd dropped a mentoring session with a junior hire because "the AI assigned me back-to-back deliverables for efficiency."

Nobody had meant harm. But the outcome was harm nonetheless.

Accountability had quietly transferred from human hands to neutral algorithms. And once handed over, it was never questioned again.

The Shadow Side of Scale

Early in a company's life, systems liberate you.

They reduce chaos. They catch the details you're too busy to see. They stabilize performance.

But at scale?

Systems start shaping behavior, often in ways you didn't intend.

People mirror the logic of the tools they use.

If a system rewards speed, the team will optimize for speed, even if it comes at the expense of nuance, reflection, or quality. If a dashboard highlights only utilization rates, people will fill their calendars, whether or not the work is meaningful. If a process values box-checking over curiosity? The boxes will get checked, and the curiosity quietly disappears.

That's the subtle power of systems. They don't just manage work. They teach people what matters.

At Innovate, Sarah had seen this pattern before. One particular internal tool tracked project progress by percentage complete. Tasks moved from red to yellow to green. Clean. Simple. Visual.

But over time, something shifted.

Projects were "green" on paper, but flat in the room. Creative energy dipped. Collaboration narrowed. Mid-level leaders started rushing to mark things as finished, not because they believed the work was complete, but because the system was watching.

Without realizing it, the firm was no longer just scaling systems. They were scaling assumptions.

Assumptions like:

- Finished equals good
- Speed equals success
- Visibility equals value
- Automation equals objectivity

And some of those assumptions, Sarah realized, were toxic.

Because they didn't just shape output. They reshaped their behavior.

Designers stopped proposing alternate approaches. PMs avoided flagging nuance if it slowed a deliverable. The team was adapting, but not in the way anyone intended.

This is the core of affordance theory in behavioral science: every tool sends a silent message about how it should be used. But in organizations, those messages become culture.[9]

Not formally. Not overtly. But slowly.

System by system. Trigger by trigger. Click by click.

So, Sarah asked the harder question. She didn't ask, "Is the system working?" She asked, "What kind of culture is this system silently creating?"

Because if you're not careful, your tools will scale the very behaviors you're trying to outgrow.

The Compliance Creep

One day, Sarah asked a junior team member how they were approaching a project hiccup.

He shrugged. "Waiting on the next status update trigger."

"Why?" she asked.

"Because the system hasn't told me to act yet."

He wasn't careless; he was following the rules.

---

9   James J. Gibson, "The Theory of Affordances," in *Perceiving, Acting, and Knowing*, ed. Robert Shaw and John Bransford (Hillsdale, NJ: Lawrence Erlbaum, 1977), 67–82.

But the rules weren't built for leadership. They were built for predictability.

That's when Sarah saw it clearly: the systems no longer serve the team. The team was serving the systems.

She pulled out her old notebook from year one. She'd once scrawled inside the cover: "Build systems that serve people, not systems that need people."

Somewhere along the way, that had flipped.

At the next executive meeting, she asked, "What's one system we maintain that takes more than it gives?"

The responses came quickly:

- The "lessons learned" tracker no one reads.
- The proposal archive, triplicated.
- A compliance doc made of copy-paste.

None of them were broken.

But all of them had outlived their purpose.

They weren't support. They were noise.

When Systems Teach the Wrong Lessons

Every system carries an implicit message, a silent signal about what matters.

Most teams never say this out loud, but they feel it.

That project tracker doesn't just organize workflow; it suggests that speed is more important than depth.

That checklist doesn't just support structure; it implies that completion is the same thing as competence.

That dashboard doesn't just display performance; it teaches that what's visible must be valuable.

Behavioral scientists call this affordance theory: A system's design subtly instructs users how to behave. Without a word, it tells people what to prioritize, avoid, and, most dangerously, what is not worth noticing.[10]

---

10   Donald A. Norman, *The Design of Everyday Things* (New York: Basic Books, 1988).

Sarah saw this unfolding across Innovate. At first, the tools were empowering. They simplified chaos, brought order to the day, and created visibility.

But slowly, something else crept in. Nuance disappeared from team huddles. Creative exploration was replaced by box-checking. The loudest incentives were about being fast, not thoughtful.

The systems weren't broken. But they were teaching the wrong lessons.

They were shaping tasks, and in doing so, they were reshaping values.

Without realizing it, Innovate had begun rewarding compliance instead of care.

People followed the process but stopped questioning whether the process still made sense. They didn't speak up, not because they didn't care, but because the system didn't ask for their judgment. It just asked for their obedience.

Complicating it all was an even deeper trap: the sunk cost fallacy. This is the human tendency to keep using a system simply because they have already invested in it. Even when it no longer served the intended purpose. Even when it quietly eroded trust. Even when it made the people using it feel more like instruments than innovators.

That was the moment Sarah realized this wasn't an operational issue. It was emotional.

The goal wasn't to force new processes. It was to invite people back into the conversation.

To rebuild systems that trusted the team to lead, not just follow. To say, "You are not a cog. You are a contributor. And your judgment is not a liability, it's an asset."

Because when systems reinforce care instead of merely compliance, culture shifts.

The Systems Reset

Sarah launched a company-wide initiative: "Liberate the Load."

Every team audited its systems, asking three questions:

Question	Intent
Who is this system really for?	Reveal blind spots in utility
What trust gap is it trying to solve?	Surface cultural wounds
What would happen if we deleted it?	Challenge fear-based rules

In just two weeks, they sunset seven systems, merged three, and revised two dashboards.

The result?

- Fewer clicks
- Fewer status updates
- More time to think.

But most importantly? People started using judgment again.

From Automation to Augmentation

Sarah reframed the company's approach to AI and software.

The question was no longer "What can we automate?" It became "Where does automation enhance judgment?"

That led to a new internal distinction:

Automation Type	Role	Outcome
Replace	Removes human input	Efficiency, but risk of drift
Recommend	Suggests action, not decision	Guidance with discretion
Reflect	Shows data to inform thinking	Insight without direction

They shifted almost all internal automation from Replace to Recommend or Reflect.

It slowed some metrics but improved decision quality and morale.

Every new technology system had to be evaluated not just on what it did, but who it was quietly training people to become.

Because tools aren't neutral. They teach.

And Sarah wanted them to teach courage, not compliance.

When Tools Break Trust

A team lead shared something that hit Sarah hard.

"Our project tool gives us all the answers, but no context. So, when someone makes a mistake, we assume they weren't paying attention, not that they were struggling."

Systems weren't just reporting reality. They were shaping their perception.

And when they removed the human context? They made it easier to assume the worst.

Absence of Context Defaults to Blame

When people lack context, they don't wait patiently for clarity. They fill in the gaps with fear, frustration, and most often, blame.

It's a deeply human reflex. The brain is wired to make meaning, especially when uncertainty creeps in. And when there's no story to explain what's happening, we create our own. Usually, it's one that protects ourselves and assigns fault to someone else.

This is why systems that abstract too much human nuance, even unintentionally, can erode trust, even on otherwise high-functioning teams.

Sarah saw this pattern emerge when Innovate's internal project dashboard began flagging delays with increasing precision. Tasks that fell behind schedule were automatically color-coded red. It was efficient. Technically accurate. But emotionally incomplete.

A junior engineer was flagged three times in one week. There was no narrative, comment box, or visible reason, just a red bar on a screen. The project manager didn't reach out; they just assumed disengagement. In truth, the engineer had been caring for a parent recovering from surgery. They were quietly doing their best and too proud to ask for accommodation.

The system wasn't trying to shame them. But in its silence, it did.

That's the danger. An absence of context defaults to blame.

When people don't know the why, they start imagining the worst. And when they don't see effort, they assume apathy.

So, Sarah made a small but powerful change she had used earlier on a late deliverables issue. She added "human notes" fields to every dashboard. A space for leaders to give context. A place for nuance. A reminder that behind every metric was a person doing their best with what they had.

The numbers didn't change. But the tone did.

Conversations softened. Managers paused before making assumptions. Team members began sharing their realities more freely. Accountability didn't vanish; it matured.

Because when systems make space for humanity, teams remember that performance isn't just data.

It's a story. It's a circumstance. It's people.

And when people feel seen, they don't need to protect themselves.

They show up fully, because they know they're being led, not just measured.

Systems Should Extend Trust, Not Replace It

They created a new mantra across the company:

"Systems should extend trust, not replace it."

That meant:

- Letting team leads override flags based on context.
- Revising SLAs to allow for creative latitude.
- Replacing "green is good" logic with "green is useful" logic.

From Rigidity to Resilience

Sarah realized the problem wasn't the systems. It was rigidity.

Systems must evolve. Flex. Respond. They can't be artifacts.

They must be living tools that grow with the culture, not freeze it.

So, she created a recurring process:

Quarterly Systems Review

System	Still useful?	What's missing?	What behavior is it creating?
Proposal generator	Partially. Needs human input restored	Creativity and design ownership	Compliance and disengagement
Lessons learned tracker	No. Replaces judgment rather than supporting it	Follow-through and reflection	Performative documentation, little learning

Every system was now a living contract, not a fixed rule.

Closing Reflection

Systems don't scale companies. People do.

And worse, there is no such thing as a neutral system.

Every platform encodes belief. Every metric implies a value. If you don't decide what the system serves, it will decide for you, and usually, it will choose speed over soul.

The only thing worse than a toxic culture is a perfect process that quietly makes people disappear.

Let your systems serve your people. Not manage them. Not optimize them.

Serve them, not surveil them.

Systems should simplify clarity, not complicate culture.

Sarah learned the hard way that good tools can still produce bad behavior when you forget the main point:

You're not building efficiency. You're building a business that works because people feel trusted, not despite it.

No process can protect the soul of a company. Only people can.

CHAPTER
08

THE TRUST
EQUATION

You Don't Scale Trust with Titles

Sarah once thought that trust came automatically with hierarchy. You earn your team's respect, get promoted, and boom, they trust you. Right?

Turns out, that's a myth.

Trust isn't about seniority. It's about consistency, clarity, and care, repeated over time, under pressure.

And as Innovate scaled, Sarah realized that trust was being quietly eroded not by bad actors but by good intentions delivered badly.

The Moment She Knew

It was during a cross-team meeting about a sensitive client request. A junior designer spoke up. "I wasn't sure if I could say something, so I just did the thing."

The thing turned out fine. But Sarah was floored.

This wasn't about the task or the request. It was about the emotional calculus behind it.

"I wasn't sure if I could" That phrase screamed low trust.

Trust Is Context-sensitive

In organizations, trust doesn't begin as a default. It's built, calibrated, and tested in motion.

People don't operate from blind belief; they read their environment like a weather system. If feedback is harsh, systems are opaque, or leadership disappears under pressure, trust doesn't just diminish; it fractures.

It becomes conditional. And once that calibration starts, even the most well-intentioned teams shift from contribution to self-protection. They withhold candor. They hesitate before offering dissent. They interpret silence not as focus, but as risk.

Because trust, like clarity, is situational. It's not defined by what you say in a values statement. It's shaped by what people experience, especially when things go sideways.

And unless your systems, signals, and leaders reinforce that trust under pressure, it will degrade. Quietly, predictably, and often, irreversibly.

The Trust Equation

Sarah went digging and found an old consulting formula she'd seen years ago:

Trust = (Credibility + Reliability + Intimacy) / Self-Orientation

It hit her like lightning.

The team trusted her to be credible and reliable, but they might not feel seen.

Maybe the intimacy, the relational part, had eroded. And maybe the self-orientation, as well as the perception that leaders were optimizing for themselves or the company, not the people, had crept up.

That one shift reframed everything. Trust isn't a vibe. It's a design decision.

So, Sarah rewrote the formula in Innovate's language.

Team Trust = (Clarity + Consistency + Connection) ÷ Perceived Self-Interest

Then she asked her leads to audit themselves:

The Trust Equation Framework

Trait	Do we model this?	Where are we slipping?
Clarity	Do people understand why decisions are made?	Dashboards replace conversations
Consistency	Are our behaviors predictable under stress?	Leaders overrule systems or default to old habits
Connection	Are we emotionally present?	Hallway conversations have decreased significantly
Self-interest	Do people believe we're in this together?	Mid-level leaders and juniors may feel excluded from shaping change

The results were humbling.

Even the best managers realized they were being clear, but not connective. They were reliable, but not warm.

Where AI Was Distorting Trust

One subtle system was contributing: their automated feedback loop.

Each week, team members could submit micro-feedback to their leads, ranked anonymously, and then shared in monthly summaries.

It was built for transparency. But it started breeding suspicion.

Some feedback felt vague. Some felt weaponized. Some team members tried to guess who said what, and trust declined.

So, they made a bold move: opt-in attribution. You could choose to attach your name or not.

Once they normalized owning feedback, trust rose. People were more thoughtful.

And people felt braver because the conversation came with context.

The Three Trust Currencies

Sarah boiled trust down into three forms of emotional currency leaders trade every day:

- Presence: Are you available when it matters?
- Prediction: Do I know how you'll respond?
- Permission: Do I feel safe to say the hard thing?

If you're bankrupt in any of those areas, your team will start protecting themselves instead of showing up.

Sarah realized that even their tools carried implications for trust.

- A dashboard that highlights underperformers without nuance? Erodes trust.
- A system that reassigns tasks midweek with no explanation? Erodes trust.
- A CRM note that calls a client "difficult" with no backup? Erodes trust.

So, they created trust filters in their internal systems.

Before any automation was pushed to people, it had to answer:

- Will this increase confidence or create anxiety?
- Will this clarify or confuse intention?
- Will this reinforce that we trust our team?

If the answer wasn't obvious, the system didn't go live until corrected.

What Trust Looks Like on the Ground

One Friday, Sarah saw something small but powerful.

A PM paused during stand-up and asked a junior engineer, "Would you do anything differently if this were your project?"

The room went still. The engineer answered. Thoughtfully. And they implemented her idea.

That moment wasn't part of any written process. It was proof of humility and trust. Proof that every voice matters, regardless of title or experience level.

Proof that trust doesn't have to be massive. It just has to be modeled.

Trust Isn't Built During All-hands Meetings. It's Built in the Hallway.

They started collecting micro-trust moments in their internal communications, one-sentence stories like:

- "Greg paused the meeting so I could finish my thought."
- "Monica gave me space to try a different client response, and it worked."
- "A senior admitted they were wrong. I'll never forget that."

They added a line to their feedback template: "Where did you feel most trusted this week?"

It became a quiet ritual, one that subtly shifted the tone of the culture.

Sarah also introduced a simple loop to help leaders rebuild trust when it was cracked:

- Name the drift.
- Acknowledge the impact.

- Co-create repair.
- Follow through visibly.

It wasn't flashy. But over time, this became the backbone of conflict recovery across teams, and it worked.

The Compounding Power of Clarity

Behavioral science shows that uncertainty isn't just uncomfortable; it's biologically exhausting.

The human brain burns far more energy processing ambiguity than it does making confident decisions.[11] Every "I'm not sure what matters most" drains creative energy and narrows collaboration.

Sarah's realization wasn't just strategic; it was neurological.

She lowered cognitive load and restored momentum without adding pressure by creating a clarity loop that was repeated, reinforced, and measured.

This is known as decision simplification: turning complex environments into repeatable emotional safety zones.

You must answer not just what to do, but why it matters. And where is it going?

The real beauty of clarity?

It compounds. Like trust, it grows faster the more consistently it's honored and requires less intervention over time.

Sarah didn't just build a system to repeat what mattered. She built a culture where people felt safe believing in it again.

The Systems That Earned Trust Back

A few quiet updates made a big difference:

- Every performance review started with, "What makes you feel seen here?"
- Project retros had a final slide: "What did we learn about trust?"
- Onboarding included a values map, real stories of moments when Innovate chose integrity over ease.

---

11   Elisabeth A. Murray and Jack Grinband, "Energy Demands Limit Our Brain's Information-Processing Capacity," *University College London News*, August 3, 2020.

These weren't gimmicks. They were culture coders. Small, deliberate signals that trust wasn't assumed, it was valued and cultivated.

Because trust doesn't scale automatically, it scales slowly, intentionally, and never through software.

It can't be delegated, and it can't be stockpiled.

It has to be earned, again and again.

Closing Reflection

Trust isn't something you "build once." It's something you model daily.

In the way you listen. The way you decide. The way you admit when you're wrong.

And when trust becomes your default operating system? Speed increases. Clarity sharpens. Retention stabilizes.

Because the most powerful performance system isn't built on pressure.

It's built on belief.

CHAPTER
09

THE CLARITY ENGINE

When Clarity Becomes Your Constraint

Sarah was tired of momentum, not in a cynical way, but in a real, worn-down-by-it kind of way.

Momentum had carried them through early growth. Through quick wins. Through new hires, new tools, and new scopes.

But now? It felt like momentum had become a runaway train. Meetings were efficient, but not deep. Projects were well-staffed but not inspired. Goals were getting hit, but nobody remembered why they mattered.

So, she asked a hard question: "What's the one thing we no longer question that we probably should?"

Monica answered instantly, "Our priorities."

That's when Sarah realized: Clarity wasn't a one-time event. It had to be a system.

Not a slide. Not a speech. Not a sentence pinned to Teams.

A system that could run without her being in every room.

Clarity Decays Under Complexity

As organizations grow, the signal-to-noise ratio doesn't just worsen; it metastasizes. Each new initiative, hire, or system adds another decibel to the hum of operational chaos.

What starts as crisp intent becomes diffused through committee edits, automated updates, and the creeping tyranny of "best practices."

Complexity multiplies. But clarity? That degrades. And here's the deeper risk: The human brain is wired for immediacy.

Urgency hijacks attention because it triggers our threat-detection systems, a neurological inheritance that evolved to prioritize short-term survival over long-term strategy. This is known as the "urgency effect": tasks that feel immediate get overvalued, even when they're less important.

So, without conscious reinforcement of what truly matters, your team won't ignore priorities; they'll simply misplace them.

Not from malice, but from overload. Because when information exceeds interpretation, we don't elevate meaning. We default to motion.

That's not failure. That's a predictable psychological response to noise disguised as progress.

The Clarity Engine

Sarah sat down with her leadership team and designed something simple:

"The Clarity Engine is a set of rituals, tools, and rules that reinforce what matters, even when things get busy."

It needed to do three things:

- Keep Vision top-of-mind.
- Translate strategy into action.
- Highlight drift before it becomes dysfunction.

They mapped it like this:

The Clarity Engine Framework

Clarity Engine Component	Function	Cadence
Vision Pulse	Reconnect team to purpose	Monthly
Priority Check	Validate real focus versus perceived	Biweekly
Drift Signals	Detect cultural or directional wobble	Ongoing
Context Layer	Add meaning to data	Embedded in tools
Feedback Loop	Capture emotional + strategic response	Quarterly

Each component became part of Innovate's new operating rhythm. Not just ideas, behaviors.

Clarity Isn't Just What You Say. It's What You Repeat.

One of Sarah's favorite phrases became their internal mantra: "If your team can't repeat your priorities without looking them up, they're not clear; they're memorized."

So, they built rituals to embed clarity.

- Every Monday, leaders restated top strategic priorities in their own words.
- Every major project had to be tied back to one of the core strategic themes.
- Every offsite began with a "why we exist" roundtable, unpolished and unprompted.

It wasn't perfect. But it was real. And it started to show.

When AI Made Clarity Worse

One small system nearly derailed the whole thing.

Their strategy team had used an AI tool to analyze project profitability and suggest adjustments. Technically, it was useful. But the suggestions lacked soul.

One project got flagged for reduced margin, and the AI recommended de-scoping a public space amenity that had a massive community impact.

The model wasn't wrong. But it wasn't right, either.

Sarah asked a powerful question: "What do we do when optimization conflicts with our identity?"

The room went silent. And that became part of the engine: a conflict clause.

Any decision, especially data or AI-driven, that contradicts the company's values must be paused and discussed live, no exceptions.

Not to slow things down. But to maintain integrity.

Clarity Killers to Watch For

They built a list of known clarity killers, patterns that creep in when momentum takes over.

Clarity Killer	Symptom	Countermeasure
Tool drift	Systems prioritize metrics over meaning	Add human context layers
Strategic drift	Projects don't ladder to goals	Biweekly priority sync
Language slippage	People use vague terms like "value" or "efficiency"	Shared language sheet
Shadow priorities	Unspoken agendas start steering action	Conflict clause invocation

This list became a self-diagnostic tool.

Each team lead reviewed it monthly with their group.

Not to catch mistakes, to stay honest.

AI-assisted Clarity: Beneficial Use Cases

Not all tech made things worse. They found three AI-enhanced workflows that reinforced clarity:

- Vision Tagging in Docs: Their internal AI assistant tagged phrases in proposals or project scopes that aligned with core values, like community impact or sustainability. It helped teams to express their intent better.

- Sentiment Trends in Stand-ups: They used Natural Language Processing (NLP) powered tools to scan weekly notes for emotional tone. If "confused" or "overwhelmed" trended, it triggered a check-in prompt.

- Pattern Highlighting in Drift Reports: Instead of flagging red metrics, the system identified pattern-level drift, i.e., when a team stopped mentioning the client's goals in their updates.

These tools didn't create clarity. But they preserved it.

Clarity Isn't a Message; It's a Muscle

The human brain is wired for meaning, but doesn't store clarity like memory. It builds it like a habit.

Cognitive psychology shows that in complex environments, salience fades fast. What was once obvious becomes background noise. This is called the clarity decay curve, where strategic focus erodes without active reinforcement.[12]

Sarah's insight was simple but profound: If clarity isn't repeated, it's replaced.

So, she didn't just build a system that made strategy visible. She built a culture where the meaning became muscle memory.

Companies that scale well don't just know what matters. They rehearse it.

Clarity Compounding Loop

Sarah realized clarity worked like compound interest. The more consistently you reinforce it, the more valuable it becomes, and the less effort it takes to maintain.

They mapped their new loop:

- Articulate: Say what matters.
- Align: Connect it to current work examples.
- Act: Let people own it.
- Audit: Ask where it's slipping.
- Adjust: Realign in real time.

Repeated. Every quarter, every project and every meeting.

This wasn't bureaucracy. It was oxygen.

Sarah noticed something surprising: the clearer their system became, the more some leaders started hiding behind it.

Instead of making hard calls, they pointed to the process.

Instead of having tough conversations, they defaulted to "what the framework says."

So, she made a distinction: "Clarity is a launchpad. Not a shield."

They started calling it clarity theater when someone used alignment language to avoid responsibility.

It was playful. But sharp. And it kept them honest.

---

12   John Sweller, "Cognitive Load During Problem Solving: Effects on Learning," *Cognitive Science* 12, no. 2 (1988): 257–285.

Final Additions to the Clarity Engine

They added one final piece:

Element	Function
"Ask Me Anything" Live Teams Thread	Founder answers open questions about purpose, direction, or tension
"What We're Not Doing" List	Visible weekly list of things being intentionally skipped
"Stories That Prove It"	A running collection of real-world examples where values guided decisions

This turned the engine from a strategy document into a cultural amplifier.

Not just for productivity. But for identity.

Closing Reflection

Clarity isn't simply understanding what matters. It's remembering, repeating, and reinforcing.

It's a rhythm, a discipline, and a design choice.

In the chaos of scale, clarity is your most renewable resource. Because when your people know what matters and why, they stop performing.

And they start building.

CHAPTER

10

CONFLICT AS A CULTURE BUILDER

The First Fight That Mattered

It started with a Teams thread. There was a simple disagreement over a scope item.

Monica suggested adding a short community survey to the preliminary site plan, a nod to their "human-first" approach.

Raj replied, flatly, "We don't have time for sentiment-gathering. Let's stick to the deliverables."

Normally, that would not have died quietly. But this time, Sarah saw the Teams messages and didn't intervene. She wanted to see what happened next. There was silence.

No one chimed in. No one resolved it. No one even acknowledged the tension.

The moment passed, but something else surfaced. They weren't disagreeing less. They were avoiding more.

And that's when Sarah realized, Innovate wasn't conflict-averse. They were conflict-illiterate.

Fear of Rupture Blocks Resilience

Teams that fear conflict don't eliminate it; they internalize it.

Research consistently shows that when conflict is seen as dangerous rather than developmental, teams don't become more aligned but become more silent.[13]

Disagreements go underground. Frustrations are repackaged as politeness. The room stays calm, but the undercurrent grows tense.

This illusion of harmony might feel like unity in the short term, but it's costly.

Over time, psychological safety erodes. Initiative dries up. Innovation stalls. And trust becomes brittle. People didn't stop caring; they just didn't feel safe enough to surface what mattered.

When rupture feels irreparable, people avoid honesty.

But resilience takes root when teams learn that rupture can lead to repair and even stronger alignment. Because resilience isn't the

---

13   Elizabeth W. Morrison and Frances J. Milliken, "Organizational Silence: A Barrier to Change and Development in a Pluralistic World," *Academy of Management Review* 25, no. 4 (2000): 706–725.

absence of friction, it's the ability to face it together without fear of breaking.

Not All Conflict Is Equal

Sarah mapped what she was seeing across teams:

Type of Conflict	Common Signs	Opportunity
Personal	Tension between individuals	Repair trust, set emotional norms
Process	Frustration with systems or workflows	Refine operations and priorities
Philosophical	Disagreements about values, direction, or "what matters"	Strengthen Vision, reveal alignment gaps

They were avoiding philosophical conflict the most, the kind that builds culture.

Because that's the kind that feels risky. But it's also the kind that refines identity.

The Cost of Peacekeeping

Peacekeeping looks noble. It sounds like leadership. But inside growing companies, it often means this:

- Agreeing publicly, then undermining privately
- Skipping tension to preserve speed
- Confusing avoidance with professionalism

Sarah saw it everywhere. Not because her team didn't care, but because they cared too much about belonging.

So, she introduced a new mantra. "Respect isn't agreement, it's engagement."

She explained it at the next team meeting. "We don't need to think the same. We need to care enough to challenge each other."

Then, she modeled it.

During the next strategy review, she openly disagreed with a direction proposed by a trusted director, with warmth, clarity, and curiosity.

No drama. No retreat. Just friction that meant something.

Conflict Handled Well Increases Psychological Safety

It's counterintuitive, but true: Teams that engage in honest, well-held conflict tend to trust each other more over time, not less.

Research shows that psychological safety deepens when disagreement is treated not as a threat but as a tool for refinement.[14]

The key is how conflict is navigated.

When leaders model curiosity over defensiveness, openness over certainty, and a willingness to be wrong, it sends a powerful signal: This is a place where truth is welcome.

That kind of environment doesn't just tolerate hard conversations; it actually invites them.

And when people know they can surface tension without risking rejection or retaliation, they stop walking on eggshells and start contributing fully.

Productive conflict becomes a form of care. A sign that the team believes the work and each other are worth the friction.

The "Disagreement Design" Workshop

Sarah ran a one-hour experiment.

Each leader wrote down one belief they held that they didn't think the rest of the team shared.

The results?

- "I don't think speed is always a virtue."
- "I'm worried we're designing too much for optics, not for outcome."
- "I think we're too polite, and it's slowing us down."

They didn't resolve everything. But something shifted.

The team finally heard each other, without the pressure to fix or defend.

---

14   Bret H. Bradley et al., "Reaping the Benefits of Task Conflict in Teams: The Critical Role of Team Psychological Safety," *Journal of Applied Psychology* 97, no. 1 (2012): 151–158.

AI, Tension, and Perceived Fairness

Interestingly, one source of hidden tension was their internal task assignment system.

It evenly distributes project hours across team members. On paper, it was fair. But in practice?

Some staff felt it disregarded passion, stretch goals, or prior project fatigue.

And no one had said anything. Not because it was a flawed system. But because they didn't know how to talk about it without sounding ungrateful.

Sarah renamed the issue "Algorithmic Resentment" and addressed it head-on.

Now, every system review asks, "Where do people feel silenced by structure?"

That question became part of their feedback rituals. And it opened conversations that no dashboard would have triggered.

The "Conflict Reframe" Practice

To normalize friction, Sarah introduced a team tool:

Conflict Avoidant Phrase	Positive Conflict Reframe
"It's probably just me, but..."	"Here's something I'm noticing"
"Let's just move forward."	"Can we pause and unpack that a bit more?"
"I don't want to make this a thing."	"I think this deserves attention."

Each team practiced these in live dialogue, not in theory.

It was awkward at first. Then powerful.

Because language gives permission, and clarity breeds courage.

Why Most Companies Skip This

Conflict training feels "extra" to most founders.

They'd rather fix the process. Invest in tools. Reassign teams.

But what they miss is this: Every cultural reset begins with a willingness to disagree out loud.

Without it, you build consensus theaters, where everything looks good until it suddenly falls apart.

Conflict Isn't a Threat, Silence Is

High-performing teams don't avoid conflict. They navigate it with intent.

Behavioral science shows that when disagreement is unsafe, people don't speak less because they agree; they speak less because they fear rupture. This is known as groupthink and voice suppression: the tendency to trade psychological safety for social acceptance.[15]

Sarah realized her team wasn't broken. They were bracing for the worst.

So, she built new norms. Disagreement became not just tolerated but expected. Philosophical friction was welcomed because that's where Vision gets stress-tested, not just stated.

Because the goal isn't to eliminate conflict, it's to design for it. Intentionally. Transparently. Together.

From Friction to Fuel

Sarah reframed conflict not as a cost, but as a source of design input.

They started capturing moments of productive tension and using them in project retrospectives.

Examples:

- "Remember when Chris pushed back on the timeline? That exposed a resource gap we hadn't spotted."
- "Raj challenging the value proposal led to the biggest BD pivot of the year."

These weren't breakdowns. They were breakthroughs.

They codified a simple three-rule charter:

- We challenge ideas, not people.
- We seek understanding, not victory.
- We repair visibly, not quietly.

---

15   Irving L. Janis, *Groupthink: Psychological Studies of Policy Decisions and Fiascoes*, 2nd ed. (Boston: Houghton Mifflin, 1982).

Every new hire reviewed it during onboarding. Every lead modeled it. Every process reinforced it.

Because culture isn't just how we get along, it's how we grow through tension.

Closing Reflection

At a leadership retreat, one team member asked, "What if we fail because we stopped disagreeing?"

That line landed.

It became shorthand for avoiding the easy way out. A reminder that friction is a feature, not a flaw.

Conflict isn't a threat to culture. It's the forge that strengthens it.

If handled with care, curiosity, and consistency, tension becomes the birthplace of clarity.

Sarah stopped fearing friction. She started designing for it. Because great companies aren't built on agreement, they're built on alignment earned through honesty.

CHAPTER
11

MAKING DECISIONS
THAT STICK

The Decision Fatigue Nobody Saw Coming

Sarah noticed the signs slowly.

Hesitation in meetings. The passive "whatever works for the team" responses. The endless need for consensus on even small choices.

It wasn't burnout. Not exactly. It was decision fatigue disguised as collaboration.

Everyone still cared. Everyone still showed up. But the edge was gone. The conviction. The willingness to say, "This is what I think, and here's why."

People were tired of choosing. Or maybe they were tired of choosing without clarity.

Repeated Ambiguity Erodes Decision Quality

The human brain isn't neutral to ambiguity; it treats it like a threat.

Neuroscience confirms that unresolved uncertainty drains cognitive energy, narrows attention, and triggers stress responses, even in low-stakes scenarios.[16]

When teams face recurring decisions without clear criteria for success, alignment fractures, people start guessing. Momentum turns into hesitancy. Eventually, ownership declines, not because people don't care, but because they're tired of choosing without a compass.

Even small tasks feel heavier when their purpose is unclear.

Over time, ambiguity becomes friction. And the more often that friction appears, the more teams default to inertia and start asking "What's safest?" instead of "What's best?"

That's why clarity isn't just a strategic advantage; it's a behavioral necessity.

Clear decisions compound. Vague ones accumulate cost.

Not All Decisions Are Created Equally

Sarah sketched a simple quadrant on the whiteboard in her office.

---

16   Shai Danziger, Jonathan Levav, and Liora Avnaim-Pesso, "Extraneous Factors in Judicial Decisions," *Proceedings of the National Academy of Sciences* 108, no. 17 (2011): 6889–6892.

Impact	Reversibility	Examples
High Impact/Hard to Reverse	Hiring execs, major clients	Needs consensus and time
High Impact/Easy to Reverse	Tool experiments, messaging shifts	Fast trial, early feedback
Low Impact/Hard to Reverse	Legal terms, long-term vendor contracts	Slow, deliberate
Low Impact/Easy to Reverse	Scheduling, internal language tweaks	Delegate and go fast

The team had been treating everything like High Impact/Hard to Reverse. No wonder they were frozen.

So, she started labeling decisions out loud. "This is a two-way door. If it doesn't work, we back out."

It was liberating.

That metaphor became part of their language.

One-way doors: choose carefully.

Two-way doors: move, learn, iterate.

Every major meeting now began with one question: "Are we opening a one-way or a two-way door?"

When AI Accelerates Indecision

The problem wasn't that they didn't have data. It was that they had too much.

One of their internal tools could simulate twenty different scenarios for any major resourcing shift. Timeline impacts. Margin forecasts. Burnout risks. Utilization trade-offs.

It was technically brilliant, but emotionally overwhelming.

Every option looked plausible. Every risk felt validated. And the more scenarios the AI surfaced, the more reluctant the team became to commit.

They called it decision paralysis by intelligence.

Eventually, Sarah drew a line: "If we need more than three data points to feel good about a move, we're not missing insight, we're missing courage."

That became a leadership rule.

Decision Fatigue and Ownership Drift

Every decision carries a cognitive cost. And when leaders are overwhelmed with complexity, that cost compounds into decision fatigue—the gradual erosion of clarity, confidence, and action.

Behavioral science shows that fatigue doesn't freeze teams. It creates avoidance behavior—endless consensus-seeking, vague approvals, and "whatever the group thinks" diplomacy.

On the surface, things look collaborative. Underneath, responsibility is dissolving.

Sarah saw it for what it was, not incompetence but protection.

Her fix wasn't more processes. It was ownership by design: clear roles, cleaner escalation paths, and the courage to let judgment live closer to the edge.

Because in uncertain terrain, the best compass isn't consensus. It's the clarity of who decides what, and when.

The Cost of False Consensus

Sarah realized something else was going wrong. To avoid conflict, leaders were chasing consensus instead of commitment.

No one was objecting, but no one was really bought in either.

So, she introduced a practice from her early startup days: disagree and commit.

It wasn't new. But it was powerful.

Leaders were encouraged to voice dissent clearly, then commit fully if the decision moved forward anyway.

This required psychological maturity and a shared understanding that disagreement was not disloyalty.

And it worked. Faster follow-through. Fewer rehashes. More resilience.

From Decision Speed to Decision Durability

Sarah reframed her goal with the team.

"I don't need us to decide faster. I need us to make decisions that stick."

That changed how they ran meetings.

- Instead of fast votes, they held tension a little longer.
- Instead of "What's the answer?" they asked, "What will we regret if we're wrong?"
- Instead of majority wins, they aimed for alignment over agreement.

Before finalizing a decision, teams answered:

- Is the rationale clear to everyone, even those who disagree?
- Have we named what we're giving up by saying yes?
- If this fails, will we still believe it was worth trying?

If they couldn't answer those? The decision wasn't ready.

A Story That Didn't Stick

Six months earlier, Sarah had signed off on a tool migration that promised to unify tasking, time tracking, and resource planning.

The demo was slick. The vendor was persuasive. The numbers penciled out.

But after rollout? Adoption tanked. People hated it.

The interface clashed with how teams actually worked. The tool created double-entry overhead. It introduced lag into conversations that had previously been handled live.

On paper, it was a good call. In practice, it failed.

But what stung more wasn't the failure. It was that no one said anything during the decision. The red flags were there, but people didn't feel they could challenge the momentum.

That became a lesson: If your team doesn't feel safe enough to stop a decision, you're not leading, you're commanding.

Who Decides What? Clarifying Discretion

To reduce confusion, they created discretion maps for each team.

Decision Type	Who Owns It	Who Must Be Consulted	Who Needs to Know
Tool selection	Ops lead	Team lead	IT

Decision Type	Who Owns It	Who Must Be Consulted	Who Needs to Know
Scope change	Project lead	Client + PM	Director
Hiring call	Hiring lead	Team + HR	Leadership

This wasn't just about efficiency. It was about confidence.

People needed to know what they could own and what they should escalate.

AI-enhanced Decision Audits

Sarah began pairing data with reflection.

They ran quarterly audits of major decisions and then had the system surface patterns:

- "You tend to delay hiring decisions longer than others."
- "Your team accepts low-margin projects thirty percent more often."
- "This department reverts to status quo eighty percent of the time."

Then leaders explained the why behind their behavior. It turned pattern-matching into strategic growth.

Revisiting Versus Rewriting

Another distinction Sarah made with her leads: "We're allowed to revisit decisions. We're not allowed to rewrite history to justify bad calls."

That meant being honest about past choices. Not covering them up. Not spinning them.

This allowed for strategic humility without cultural shame.

Why Decisions Don't Stick

Sarah identified five root causes of decision decay:

Root Cause	Symptom	Solution
Lack of clarity	People keep asking what we're doing	Clarify purpose and constraints

Root Cause	Symptom	Solution
Lack of alignment	Passive agreement, private disagreement	Hold space for dissent
Emotional misread	The team isn't ready, even if the logic is sound	Pause for pulse checks
Premature closure	No time to explore risks	Add a "What could go wrong?" layer
Process ambiguity	"Who decides?" confusion	Use discretion maps

They reviewed this list monthly, not because they feared failure but because they respected the cost of confusion.

Team Trust and Reversible Mistakes

Sarah coached her leaders on this mindset: "If we can't afford for someone to make a decision, we haven't trained them, we've trapped them."

This built the foundation for a risk-resilient decision culture. One where junior staff could try, learn, and own. One where reversibility was a strength, not a sign of weak planning.

The real test came during a client crisis. Late changes. Legal exposure. Budget threat.

The team looked to Sarah. She paused. "This is a one-way door," she said. "Let's slow down. What will we wish we'd protected if this goes south?"

That reframing slowed the panic. It surfaced real fears. And it led to a better, if harder, decision.

Closing Reflection

Good decisions aren't just smart. They're felt, owned, and reinforced.

Sarah learned that scalable leadership doesn't mean making perfect calls. It means building a culture where people think clearly, speak honestly, and choose courage over comfort, again and again.

Because when your people know how to decide and believe in what they've decided, they'll carry the weight. And carry it well.

CHAPTER
12

LEADERSHIP IS A SYSTEM

The Myth of the Natural Leader

Sarah used to believe great leaders were born that way.

Charisma. Confidence. Clarity. You either had it or you didn't.

It was a comforting story, until she realized it wasn't helping her company scale.

The reality hit during a quarterly check-in with one of her strongest mid-level managers. The metrics were fine. Morale was fine. But the energy? Gone.

The manager said it simply, "I don't know what kind of leader you want me to be."

That sentence cracked something open.

It wasn't a lack of skill. It wasn't a lack of tools. It was a lack of definition.

The company had built workflows, tech stacks, and hiring funnels, but hadn't built a leadership system. Without one, people were guessing, or worse, performing.

Leadership Shouldn't Be a Personality Test

Sarah looked across her organization and saw five styles of leadership in play:

- The Doer: leads by example, burns out silently.
- The Cheerleader: energizes others, avoids conflict.
- The Strategist: makes smart moves, stays emotionally distant.
- The Servant: beloved, but overloaded
- The Enforcer: gets stuff done but erodes trust.

Each had strengths. But none were complete. And none were coherent across the organization.

So, she asked a new question: "What if leadership wasn't a personality, but a system?"

Systematizing Leadership Restores Identity

When leadership isn't defined, people don't stop leading; they just start guessing. And guessing, over time, creates role fatigue: the emotional exhaustion caused by self-monitoring, second-guessing, and constantly interpreting unspoken expectations.

Behavioral science shows that people who lack psychological safety tend to perform instead of lead. They mimic what they think is expected instead of modeling what the organization actually needs.[17]

Sarah realized that without shared structure, even the best leaders eventually burn out, not from the workload but from the identity load.

Her breakthrough wasn't a checklist. It was a behavioral backbone, a common language that allowed leaders to show up consistently, courageously, and without losing themselves in the process.

Because real leadership isn't just visible. It's repeatable and safe to grow into.

What Systems Do for Teams, They Must Also Do for Leaders

Sarah realized they needed the same things for leadership that they demanded from project planning:

- Shared language
- Visible rhythms
- Measurable signals
- Scalable feedback

So, she began building the Leadership System.

Not a checklist. A living design.

Sarah worked with her directors to co-create five behavioral pillars that would define leadership at every level.

Pillar	Description
Clarity	Defines direction, sets expectations, names what matters
Connection	Builds trust, sees the individual, listens deeply
Coaching	Grows others, gives feedback, shares authority
Accountability	Owns outcomes, honors integrity, resolves tension
Modeling	Lives the culture visibly, especially under pressure

They weren't aspirational traits. They were practices.

And every leader could start doing them today.

---

17   Amy C. Edmondson, "Psychological Safety and Learning Behavior in Work Teams," *Administrative Science Quarterly* 44, no. 2 (1999): 350–383.

From Traits to Behaviors

Instead of asking "Are you a strong leader?" Sarah's team now asked:

- "How have you enhanced clarity this week?"
- "Where did you choose connection over speed?"
- "What coaching moment are you most proud of?"
- "What did you own that wasn't technically your fault?"
- "When did you model our values under stress?"

Leadership wasn't about vibe anymore. It was about visible, repeatable actions.

Leadership Health > Leadership Heroics

Sarah realized that many of her best leaders were compensating for system gaps.

They were staying late to fix handoffs, softening bad decisions from above, and quietly patching cultural missteps.

Heroic? Maybe. Sustainable? Not even close.

So, she created the Leadership Load Audit.

Leader	Task absorbed that isn't theirs	Why?	Impact if they stop?	System fix needed?
Monica	Shielded a junior staff from client requests	Avoided escalation fatigue	Junior staff feel exposed	Client expectation setting
Raj	Finalized proposals without design input	Believed that it's faster	Designers feel disempowered	Proposal process re-integration
Greg	Covered up missed deadlines silently	Didn't want to trigger escalation	False confidence in dashboard data	Delay transparency trigger

This shifted the narrative from "Who's falling short?" to "What's the system asking of people that it shouldn't?"

It wasn't about blame. It was about design.

One uncomfortable insight? They were using dashboards as a proxy for leadership presence.

Instead of asking, "How's your team feeling?" leaders were checking team sentiment metrics.

Instead of calling someone who missed a deliverable, they logged a system flag and waited.

The software wasn't wrong, but it also wasn't relational.

So, they rewrote the playbook: "AI can monitor, but it can't care."

Now, for every AI insight, a human follow-up was expected.

If someone's sentiment score dropped, the leader called.

If a notification fired for utilization, the question was, "How are you doing?"

Leadership returned to eye level.

Leadership Systems Don't Replace Judgment. They Shape It.

Sarah's team rolled out a set of leadership rituals tied to the five pillars.

Pillar	Weekly Practice
Clarity	Restate priorities in your own words at team meetings
Connection	One 1:1 conversation not about work
Coaching	Spot one small opportunity to delegate or teach
Accountability	Name and own one visible decision or mistake
Modeling	Reflect publicly on a leadership moment that stretched you

No one was expected to be perfect. But everyone was expected to practice.

Leadership Identity Is Built Through Small Visible Behaviors, Not Role Titles

Titles don't define leadership; it's demonstrated in moments.

Teams don't calibrate their understanding of leadership based on org charts or slide decks. They learn it by observation. They understand who speaks up when something's off, who takes responsibility when stakes are high, and who leans in when clarity is low.

People are watching not for perfection but for pattern, especially in moments of pressure, ambiguity, or discomfort. And what they see, either consistently or inconsistently, becomes the culture.

A system that reinforces those small, visible acts of leadership builds coherence. Not just around who's "in charge," but around what being a leader actually means.

In healthy cultures, leadership is less about hierarchy and more about habit. Especially those habits that are visible, repeatable, and aligned with the values the organization claims to hold.

Promotions Based on Pillars

Perhaps the biggest shift? Leadership advancement was now tied to how well someone demonstrated the five pillars, not just project success.

This changed everything.

People who coached others were noticed. Those who modeled values were promoted, not just the ones who "got things done."

Leadership became something to grow into, not something handed out.

Three months in, a big project went sideways. A client changed specs. An estimate had errors. A junior team member was feeling the pressure.

It could've become a blame spiral. Instead?

- The lead restated the mission clearly (Clarity)
- Held a non-defensive check-in with the team (Connection)
- Gave the junior space to course-correct (Coaching)
- Owned the estimate miss to the client (Accountability)

- Shared the learning company-wide (Modeling)

It wasn't smooth.

But it was systemic. And it showed everyone what leadership looked like under pressure.

Leadership Is Teachable. But Only If It's Visible.

Sarah stopped asking herself if people were "natural leaders." She started asking if they were practicing leadership consistently, with support.

That meant:

- Feedback loops
- Language for what good looks like
- Safe space to fail upward.
- A culture that values impact over ego

And most importantly? A system that never forgets that every leader is a mirror.

Closing Reflection

Leadership isn't a vibe, and it's not charisma. It's not bravado, and it's not the loudest voice in the room.

It's a rhythm. A practice. A system.

And when you design for it?

You don't just grow managers. You grow a company where everyone leads a little better every day.

Because leadership isn't a crown you earn, it's a habit you build.

CHAPTER

13

CULTURE IS WHAT YOU REINFORCE

The Invisible Engine

The most dangerous culture problems Sarah had faced were never the loud ones.

Not the heated feedback. Not the missed deadlines. Not even the performance issues.

It was a quiet drift.

The moments when good people started defaulting to "good enough."

When meetings became efficient but empty.

When the language changed from "we believe" to "we deliver."

There was no scandal. No crisis. Just erosion.

Of energy, clarity, and especially of belief.

And that's when Sarah wrote a sentence in her notebook: "Culture is not what you say. It's what you reward, and what you ignore."

Reinforcement > Aspiration

Culture doesn't drift because people forget what you said. It drifts because they respond to what you actually reward.

In behavioral psychology, operant conditioning is the principle that behavior follows reinforcement, not intention.[18] Add to that expectancy theory, and you get a dangerous loop. If people believe values-aligned actions aren't recognized, they slowly stop doing them.[19]

Sarah's team hadn't abandoned the culture. They'd stopped believing it mattered.

The fix wasn't a new set of values. It was a new spotlight, one that made the quiet alignment moments visible—small, daily proof that "what we say" is still who we are.

Because in every company, culture isn't what's declared. It's what's demonstrated, especially when nobody's watching.

18   B. F. Skinner, *The Behavior of Organisms: An Experimental Analysis* (New York: Appleton-Century, 1938).
19   Victor H. Vroom, *Work and Motivation* (New York: Wiley, 1964).

The Culture Audit Nobody Expected

Sarah called a meeting with her leadership team and opened with one question: "What are we reinforcing by accident?"

They paused. Then the answers came.

- "We praise speed more than strategy."
- "We celebrate client satisfaction more than employee boundaries."
- "We reward heroics but never reflect on why they were needed."
- "We assume culture is fine unless someone quits."

None of it was malicious. It was just unexamined.

So, Sarah proposed a shift: "Let's build a reinforcement system, on purpose."

Culture Isn't a Vibe. It's a System of Signals.

Every company has cultural inputs:

- The stories that get told
- The people who get promoted
- The Teams reactions that get clicked
- The behaviors that get modeled, or ignored

Sarah mapped out the main cultural signals across Innovate:

Signal	Current Behavior	Unintended Message
Meeting tone	All business, no check-ins	Efficiency > humanity
Promotion criteria	Based on output, not collaboration	Lone wolves get ahead
Recognition	Focused on big wins	Everyday integrity isn't visible
Tools	Reward utilization metrics	People = resources, not humans

From Accidental to Intentional Culture

They rebuilt these cultural moments, one by one.

- Meetings now began with a human check-in.
- Performance reviews included values and behaviors.
- Weekly recognition included "unsung moments of alignment."
- Dashboards added emotional signals, not just deadlines.

It wasn't a rebrand. It was a repatterning.

The Behavior Spotlight

Sarah introduced a weekly ritual: the Behavior Spotlight.

Each Friday, one person would share an example of a teammate living the company's values, even if it wasn't flashy.

The first week? A junior designer shared how a senior manager stopped a meeting to inquire about her opinion and used her insight in the final design.

The team applauded.

More importantly? The manager blushed. And said, "I didn't think anyone noticed."

That's how culture lives, not in policy but in pattern.

What's repeated becomes real.

Sarah kept AI in the loop, but with limits.

Their system could surface patterns of collaboration, even tone of voice trends in written communications. It flagged things like:

- Positive sentiment drop in a department
- Feedback avoidance trends
- Over-utilization of a few "culture carriers"

But instead of automating action, it triggered a human inquiry.

The prompt wasn't "Fix this."

It was "Who's quietly holding your culture together right now, and are they okay?"

Culture Carriers Are Not Infinite

They discovered something subtle and dangerous.

The same people who were most aligned with the company's values were also burning out the fastest.

Why? Because they were compensating for structural gaps:

- Smoothing conflict
- Filling empathy voids
- Mentoring without bandwidth
- Being "the good energy" every day

So, Sarah created the Culture Load Map:

Name	Known cultural contributions	Role	At risk of burnout?	How are we supporting them?
Monica	Mentorship, coaching junior staff	Operations	Yes	Currently informal; needs formal mentorship credit
Raj	Community storytelling, Vision reframing	Design Lead	Moderate	Included in strategic planning but lacks structured time for narrative work
Greg	Process stability, conflict de-escalation	Project Management	Yes	Not yet supported; needs risk flag visibility and shared escalation structure

This helped them redistribute care, not just responsibility.

Culture Isn't Set at the Top. It's Shaped at the Edge.

One of Sarah's favorite practices came from a project team.

They started each project kickoff with two prompts:

- "What part of our culture do we want to protect during this work?"
- "What behaviors might be tested under pressure?"

It was simple, but incredibly powerful.

It normalized vulnerability before friction.

Stories as Scaffolding

To make culture stick, they doubled down on storytelling. They created a company-wide "Proof of Culture" archive—short, real stories of values in action.

Examples included:

- A lead pausing to resolve a conflict mid-client call.
- A team overruling a profitable but values-misaligned pitch.
- A junior engineer owning a mistake without fear of punishment.
- A PM making space for grief when a teammate lost a loved one.

They shared these stories monthly.

Not as PR. As reinforcement.

Because behavior changes when the brain sees itself in the narrative.

The Culture Flywheel

Over time, Sarah saw a pattern emerging, a flywheel of how culture actually sustained itself:

- Clarity: People know what we believe.
- Visibility: They see it modeled.
- Recognition: They feel it matters.
- Practice: They act it out.
- Story: The action becomes a shared memory.
- Reinforcement: The memory becomes a signal.

And then back to clarity.

Each layer built an emotional infrastructure. Not noise. Not fluff. Resilience.

Emotional Consistency Creates Cultural Security

Culture doesn't require perfection. It requires predictability.

People don't trust an organization because every moment feels good. They trust it because the emotional tone remains stable, even when things get hard.

When leaders behave in alignment with stated values, especially under pressure, it sends a signal: This place is safe not just when we succeed, but when we struggle.

That kind of emotional consistency creates what I call "cultural security." a concept rooted in findings from behavioral psychology showing that people thrive when rules feel fair, feedback is constructive, and risk is not punished arbitrarily.[20]

In that environment, people don't waste energy scanning for signals of danger. They use that energy to focus, contribute, and stretch.

Over time, a consistent emotional tone becomes a performance multiplier, not because people fear failure, but because they believe they'll be seen fairly when it happens.

The Culture Missteps That Almost Cost Them

Sarah was transparent about the misses, too. They'd once rolled out a "values bonus" program to all employees complete with metrics, points, and nominations.

It backfired.

People gamified it. Left sincere moments unspoken. Created competitive friction.

The intention was good. The design was broken.

The lesson?

---

20   Amy C. Edmondson, *The Fearless Organization: Creating Psychological Safety in the Workplace for Learning, Innovation, and Growth* (Hoboken, NJ: Wiley, 2019).

You can't incentivize everyone into integrity. You have to create space for meaning.

Sarah had seen strong results with middle leaders by highlighting "cultural impact" wins. But here, she learned the hard way that not every playbook transfers from one setting to another.

Closing Reflection

Culture isn't about what you say. It's about what people repeat when you're not in the room.

It's what gets applauded, whispered about, and remembered.

Sarah stopped trying to craft a perfect culture. She started reinforcing the real one every week, during every meeting, with every quiet little signal that said:

"This is who we are. This is what we protect. And this is what we build, together."

Because culture isn't just the soil we plant in, it's the air we breathe.

And it's up to us to keep it clean.

CHAPTER
14

FOUNDATIONS THAT SCALE

The Final Question

Sarah stared at the whiteboard in the conference room, the one they'd used for years. It was still stained with the ghost of old timelines, names, and plans.

The team was gone. The office was quiet. The whiteboard behind her still held the scrawled headline from that morning's session: Legacy Vision: What We're Leaving Behind.

She stared at it for twenty minutes. Then erased it.

She hadn't liked any of the answers.

Sarah had seen this pattern before. Founders drafting noble phrases while secretly clinging to the comfort of control, the seduction of scale, and the image of impact.

Earlier that day, Greg had asked her a hard question. "We're aligned again. The systems are better. The team's stepping up. So, what do you want now?"

She hadn't answered because she didn't know. Not anymore.

The game had changed. She was no longer the essential bottleneck. The culture no longer bent around her moods. The machine didn't need her to run, but it did need her to choose.

Not a strategy. A stance.

Innovate had become a real company. And now it had to become a lasting one.

Because growth is what founders chase, but scaling, that's a different beast.

Scaling means what you build holds up when you're not in the room. And that means your foundation matters more than your firepower.

It's when you realized that what got us here won't take us there.

The early stages of a company are built on proximity. You see everything. You touch everything. You react in real time. But what happens when you step back? What happens when your systems, tools, and people start leading without you?

That's when cracks show.

- Culture becomes vague.
- Strategy becomes reactive.

- Tools become noise.

- Leadership becomes siloed.

- Teams start following the process instead of the purpose.

Sarah knew the feeling. She'd lived it. And that's what this entire book, this entire journey, had taught her:

Founders don't scale businesses. They engineer the foundations that they can scale upon.

Most books like this end with clarity, triumph, succession.

But real legacy isn't triumphant. It's complicated.

It's a messy mix of wins you didn't plan, costs you didn't notice, and people who outgrew you while you were too busy "leading."

Legacy, Sarah realized, might not be what you design, but what you're willing to leave unfinished so others can finish it better.

Sarah walked back to her desk. Pulled out a sticky note.

Wrote seven words: "Would they still build it without me?"

She stared at it, left it on her chair, and walked out.

Sustainable Organizations Scale Identity, Not Just Output

Enduring companies aren't defined by how much they produce but by how clearly they know who they are.

Growth without identity is just expansion. It stretches capacity but leaves culture brittle.

In contrast, organizations that scale with intention embed belief into behavior. They design systems, rituals, and decisions that reinforce who they are, not just what they do.

That's the real test of sustainability: When the founder steps back, does the mission still appear in the room? If the answer is yes, identity has scaled. If the answer is silence or drift, the culture was never built to carry the weight.

Sustainable organizations hardwire their "why" into hiring, leading, deciding, and delivering.

Output matters, but without identity, it fades. Because volume alone doesn't create legacy. Values do.

Foundation ≠ Rigidity

Sarah used to think "foundations" meant locked-in, permanent structures. But now, she saw it differently.

A strong foundation doesn't trap you. It frees you.

Like a trellis for a growing vine, it provides shape without stifling movement.

A real foundation does three things:

- Preserves identity.
- Distributes clarity.
- Inspires adaptation.

The Identity Loop

Foundations don't scale because they're strong. They scale because they're self-reinforcing.

Behavioral science shows that when people see themselves in the system, roles reflect values, and actions shape meaning, they protect it.[21]

This is the identity loop: the cycle where belief shapes behavior, and behavior reaffirms belief.

Sarah had finally closed that loop. Not by locking everything in. But by building enough clarity to trust and enough adaptability to grow. Because systems alone don't sustain a company.

People perform well when they believe in what they've been invited to build.

Looking Back: What They Built

1. Culture → From Vibes to Values-In-Action

They moved from aspirational posters to daily behaviors, feedback systems, storytelling, and rituals.

They learned that culture isn't declared; it's demonstrated. And it's only as real as what gets repeated.

2. Leadership → From Personality to Practice

They built a system for what leadership looks like across every level.

---

21   Blake E. Ashforth and Fred Mael, "Social Identity Theory and the Organization," *Academy of Management Review* 14, no. 1 (1989): 20–39.

Not titles. Not traits. But daily, teachable behaviors that are tied to clarity, connection, accountability, and modeling.

3. Decision-making → From Bottlenecks to Belief-Based Autonomy

They learned that speed isn't the prize. Durability is.

They replaced ambiguity with discretion maps. Implemented "two-way door" language. Used AI to reflect patterns, not dictate outcomes.

They stopped chasing the fastest call and started investing in the right one.

4. Systems → From Efficiency to Empowerment

Their tools stopped replacing judgment and started augmenting it.

They stripped out deadweight systems. Turned data into conversation. Made context visible again.

Because tech is only useful when it strengthens trust, not just output.

5. Scaling → From Stress to Strength

They stopped glorifying growth for its own sake. And started asking: "Are we building something that holds under pressure?"

Not everything was faster. But everything was clearer.

What They Let Go

Every growth curve has a shadow, a set of beliefs you have to shed to evolve.

Old Belief	New Belief
We have to say yes to stay afloat	We say yes to stay aligned
Process is the enemy of creativity	Process, done right, protects space to create
Good people figure it out	Good systems let good people thrive
Culture happens naturally	Culture is reinforced or it erodes
Tools fix problems	Tools amplify what's already working or failing

These shifts weren't academic. They were earned through mistakes and friction. Real human feedback.

AI as a Mirror, Not a Leader

Looking back, you can see Innovate's AI journey clearly.

They had initially used it to replace work, then to accelerate decisions.

But its most powerful role?

To reveal patterns. To surface bias. To show drift. To catch friction points early.

But AI was never the leader. It was a mirror, showing them what they might not have seen.

The real leadership? Still human. Still hard. Still worth it.

Tech Doesn't Reduce Leadership Burden; it Clarifies Where It's Most Needed

Technology isn't a substitute for leadership; it's a spotlight.

The best systems don't eliminate the emotional signals that matter; they surface them.

When tools are designed to reveal, not replace, what people are feeling, struggling with, or avoiding, leaders are better positioned to act with clarity.

Rather than drowning in noise, they can focus on what matters most: moments of friction, patterns of disengagement, and subtle cues of burnout or misalignment. Instead of reacting to metrics, they can respond to meaning.

This kind of tech-enabled awareness doesn't reduce the leadership load; it refines it.

It allows leaders to show up where they're most needed: not everywhere, but intentionally.

With more empathy. With better timing. With deeper impact. Because the goal isn't to automate leadership, it's to sharpen its aim.

A Founder's Real Job

Sarah now saw her role not as the visionary. Not as the problem-solver. Not even as the culture keeper.

Her real job? To build the foundation that others could stand on and trust.

She didn't need to be everywhere and she didn't need to know everything.

She just had to make sure the right beliefs were built into the bones of the company.

So even when she was gone, the mission wouldn't be.

What Foundations That Scale Have in Common

As Innovate stabilized, Sarah documented what worked, not just for her but for the dozens of founder-led firms she'd collaborated with over the years.

Foundation Element	What It Requires	What It Protects
Vision	Repetition, story, clarity	Purpose and cohesion
Culture	Feedback, modeling, rituals	Trust and belonging
Systems	Simplicity, discretion, empathy	Energy and resilience
Leadership	Practice, visibility, accountability	Momentum and alignment
Decision-Making	Time, courage, transparency	Confidence and ownership
Conflict Design	Safety, clarity, coaching	Integrity and truth
Scaling Strategy	Boundaries, filters, belief	Mission over vanity

These were the pillars. The invisible infrastructure that made scale sustainable.

Not perfect. Not frictionless. But real.

What She Tells New Founders Now

When new founders ask Sarah how to scale, she doesn't start with tech stacks.

She asks:

- What part of your business can't survive without you?
- What beliefs are baked into your processes?
- Who do you trust to challenge your decisions, and are they doing it?
- What would your team say you reinforce most consistently?

And then she says:

"You're not building a company. You're building a system of belief. And systems of belief, when reinforced, can survive anything."

The Foundation Lives in the Rituals

Sarah's calendar still holds reminders.

- First Monday: "Ask your team what you're ignoring."
- Mid-month Friday: "Celebrate the moment nobody saw."
- Quarterly kickoff: "Remind them what matters. Then ask what matters to them."
- Annual offsite: "Review the foundation. Don't build on sand."

These aren't to-do items. They're anchors.

They quietly hold the structure in place so the team can do what they were built to do: build, create, lead, and grow.

Closing Reflection

This isn't a book about infrastructure. It's not about dashboards or SOPs or slick leadership tricks. It's about the deep, invisible structures that actually make a company strong.

Trust.

Clarity.

Belief.

And the courage to reinforce those things, even when growth screams for shortcuts.

Foundations don't get press releases. They don't go viral on social media. But they hold the weight. Silently.

This book isn't ending with an answer. Because leadership never does.

You don't get a clean legacy. You get choices. Habits. Systems.

And one last, enduring question: Are you building something that deserves to outlive your presence?

If not, now's the time to start on purpose.

ACKNOWLEDGEMENTS

No legacy is built alone.

This book is a reflection of the many quiet, courageous conversations I've had with founders who dared to ask deeper questions, not just about growth but about meaning.

Thank you to the entrepreneurs, builders, and leaders who shared their conference rooms, whiteboards, and real, raw doubts with me. Your trust shaped these pages more than you know.

To the clients who invited me behind the curtain, not for the press or praise, but to build something better together, this book is as much yours as mine. You reminded me that integrity can scale, and culture can endure.

To the teams I've worked alongside, who brought vision to life one decision at a time, you are proof that strategy without soul is just noise.

To the mentors and friends who challenged me to write what was true, not just what was trendy, your fingerprints are on every chapter.

To my family and friends, who offered both patience and perspective during late nights and early drafts, you are my foundation.

And to you, the reader: If you've made it here, you're not just building a company. You're building a legacy. Thank you for caring enough to lead with clarity and doing the deep work when it matters most.

The world needs what you're building.

ABOUT THE AUTHOR

Jamie DeWispelare believes the greatest companies in the world aren't built in Silicon Valley. They're built in conference rooms that smell like whiteboard ink and last night's coffee.

For over twenty years, Jamie has collaborated with the founders who don't just scale revenue; they scale trust. Builders. Designers. Engineers. People who didn't inherit empires but created blueprints for something that needed to exist.

He's been the quiet voice in the room when clarity disappeared. The one who asks the harder question. The one who reminds leaders that momentum without meaning is just motion.

As a seasoned finance executive, leadership advisor, and optimization consultant, Jamie has guided first-generation founders through the toughest transitions of their business lives: from being the hero to building a system that doesn't need one. From gut decisions to intentional design. From survival to significance.

His gift is helping leaders build what lasts without losing what matters. And if you ask him what scaling really means?

Growth doesn't change who you are. It reveals it.

So, you'd better build on purpose.